THE UNOFFICIAL
MICHELLE OBAMA
ACTIVITY BOOK

Nathan Joyce

Illustrations by Toby Triumph

STERLING

New York

STERLING
New York

An Imprint of Sterling Publishing Co., Inc.
1166 Avenue of the Americas
New York, NY 10036

ISBN 978-1-4549-3823-1

Distributed in Canada by Sterling Publishing Co., Inc.
c/o Canadian Manda Group, 664 Annette Street
Toronto, Ontario M6S 2C8, Canada

For information about custom editions, special sales, and premium and corporate purchases, please contact Sterling Special Sales at 800-805-5489 or specialsales@sterlingpublishing.com.

Printed in Singapore

1 2 3 4 5 6 7 8 9 10

sterlingpublishing.com

CONTENTS

Introduction

Last year, I wrote a book like this about David Attenborough. So, with this book on Michelle, it's dawned on me that I'm working through my dream dinner party guest list. I may leave my Charles Darwin activity book idea until last though.

Michelle Obama is a remarkable person—an inspirational, compassionate, forward-thinking, brave, brilliant person. The words she chooses and the subjects she discusses affect people all over the world, breaking down barriers and normalizing topics that others have been scared to talk about. She's not afraid to talk about issues and circumstances that have affected her, but that's one of the reasons why we love her so much. Like us, she's a real person, who encounters real bumps in the road, but it's the way that she navigates them, with candor, warmth and sincerity, that earn our respect. As a repressed Brit, I owe her a debt of gratitude.

Who can forget the story of Michelle bringing in newborn Sasha to a job interview, simultaneously explaining why a flextime position may be a good way to go, while bouncing Sasha on her lap and praying her diaper remained in place? Or giving the Secret Service the slip, sneaking out to the White House lawn with Malia so she could see the White House lit up in the rainbow hues of the Pride flag?

So I've hatched a plan: invite Michelle over to accept an honorary doctorate at the University of Westminster in London. Convince her that the ceremony takes place at 10 Downing Street. Open the door, give her the scroll, shut the door, and run away. Congratulations, Michelle! This is your new home, and new job. I'm sure Barack will understand—you've got credit in the bank!

Plan B. Send Michelle an official invite to meet the Queen again. Entirely plausible—they hit it off last time. Present Michelle with the visitor's book to sign, commemorating her visit. Only it's not a visitor's book at all—it's an "adjustment" to the legal line of succession. Charles will be fine. His Duchy of Cornwall's biscuit line is doing terribly well. Long live Queen Michelle!

Anyway, I hope you enjoy this silly book. You'll laugh, you'll learn extraordinary things about Michelle, and you may even occupy the kids for a bit. Although hopefully you won't begin every sentence with "You know, Michelle says…" and "Michelle let Barack go to Bali for six weeks to finish his book," which my wife is still putting up with.

This a celebration of Michelle's life. And it feels like she's only just getting started!

Hope

"I am an example of what is possible when girls from the very beginning of their lives are loved and nurtured by people around them."

G20 SUMMIT, LONDON, 2009

"Don't ever make decisions based on fear. Make decisions based on hope and possibility. Make decisions based on what should happen, not what shouldn't."

CAMPAIGNING IN PHOENIX, ARIZONA, 2008

"Barack and I were both raised by families who didn't have much in the way of money or material possessions but who had given us something far more valuable—their unconditional love, their unflinching sacrifice, and the chance to go places they had never imagined for themselves."

AT THE DEMOCRATIC NATIONAL CONVENTION, 2012

"It is our fundamental belief in the power of hope that has allowed us to rise above the voices of doubt and division, of anger and fear, that we have faced in our own lives and the life of this country. Our hope that if we work hard enough and believe in ourselves, we can be whatever we dream, regardless of the limitations that others may place on us."

AT A CEREMONY HONORING THE 2017 SCHOOL COUNSELOR OF THE YEAR

WORLD RECORD HOLDER

- On October 11, 2011, Michelle helped set a Guinness World Record for the most people doing jumping jacks (also known as star jumps) in a 24-hour period.

- The record-breaking attempt was organized in association with National Geographic Kids to support Michelle's Let's Move! initiative, aimed at ensuring kids stay active and eat well. Michelle joined 400 local children on the South Lawn of the White House, performing one minute of continuous jumping jacks, which signaled the start of the 24-hour period.

- In total, **300,265 people** across the world participated in 1,050 different locations, smashing the previous record of 20,424. Congratulations, Michelle!

- Michelle said with characteristic cheerfulness: "I get to do a lot of cool things, but this is really exciting. I never thought in my entire life that I would be here today to break a Guinness World Record. Woohoo!"

SPECIES NAMED AFTER THE OBAMAS

LASIOGLOSSUM OBAMAI

Thirteen species of fauna and flora have been named after Barack and one species after both Barack and Michelle. Although, if I were Michelle, I wouldn't be that jealous of having two parasitic flatworms being named after me. Or an orange sea slug for that matter.

They're catching up with David Attenborough, who's sitting pretty* on twenty species and one genus. Still some way from Charles Darwin and Alexander von Humboldt, though, alas.

* No animals have been hurt by David Attenborough ever.

SPECIES NAME	DESCRIPTION	DATE
APTOSTICHUS BARACKOBAMAI	Trapdoor spider endemic to California	December 2012
BARACKTREMA OBAMAI	Parasitic flatworm found in Malaysian turtles	September 2016
CALOPLACA OBAMAE	Lichen species discovered on Santa Rosa Island in California	March 2009
DESMOPACHRIA BARACKOBAMAI	Diving beetle from French Guiana	April 2015
ETHEOSTOMA OBAMA	Perch-like fish endemic to Tennessee	November 2012
LASIOGLOSSUM OBAMAI	Large bee from Cuba	July 2016
NYSTALUS OBAMAI	Tree dwelling insectivorous bird from the Amazon	August 2013
OBAMADON GRACILIS	Extinct lizard from the Late Cretaceous in North America	December 2012
OBAMUS CORONATUS	600-million-year-old ridged, disc-shaped organism found in southern Australia	June 2018
PARAGORDIUS OBAMAI	Parasitic Kenyan flatworm	April 2012
PLACIDA BARACKOBAMAI	Pale orange sea slug found in Hawaii	October 2017
SPINTHARUS BARACKOBAMAI	Cuban smiley-faced spider	September 2017
TELEOGRAMMA OBAMAORUM	Fish from the Congo, named in honor of Barack and Michelle's commitment to education and conservation in Africa	April 2015
TOSANOIDES OBAMA	Pink, blue, and yellow coral reef fish discovered in the Papahānaumokuākea Marine National Monument in Hawaii	June 2016

Early Years

- Michelle LaVaughn Robinson was born to Marian Shields and Fraser Robinson III in Chicago on January 17, 1964.

- Her father was a pump operator for the city water department. In his spare time, he worked as a precinct captain for the Democratic Party, bringing Michelle along to meetings with constituents. He passed on feedback to the elected alderman who controlled the ward.

- Michelle's mother, Marian, was a homemaker until Michelle entered high school, when she found a job as an executive assistant in a bank. She later worked as a secretary in the office of a catalog company.

- Michelle and her older brother Craig, who are two years apart, were initially brought up in an affordable housing apartment built in the 1950s for black working-class families.

- When Michelle was a toddler, her parents accepted an offer to move a few miles south to the South Side of Chicago to share a bungalow with Marian's Aunt Robbie and her husband.

- Marian, Fraser, Michelle, and Craig shared a space designed as an in-law apartment. Michelle and Craig held brother–sister boxing matches in the kitchen, played Jackson 5 records on the sound system, and sprayed furniture polish on the floor so they could slide around in their socks.

- Michelle's grandfather, Purnell "Southside" Shields, inspired Michelle's passion for music, especially for jazz. He bought Michelle her first album—Stevie Wonder's *Talking Book,* which he kept on a special shelf he set aside for Michelle's favorite records.

- Craig began to develop anxieties about catastrophes befalling him. When he became worried about losing his sight, he wore a blindfold around the house to help him prepare. And, worried about amputation, he learned how to do his homework with his right arm behind his back.

- Craig's biggest fear was fire, so he elected himself family fire marshal and ran full-scale fire drills at home. Michelle was his lieutenant, tasked with clearing the exits. Craig would order their father to lie limp on the floor, as if he'd passed out from smoke inhalation, and would then practice dragging him to the stairs.

- Fraser and Marian bought Michelle and Craig a set of the *Encyclopedia Britannica* and a dictionary. Any time the kids had a question about a word, a concept or a historic event, they provided the kids with the answer.

Rosie the Riveter

In 1943, J. Howard Miller designed a wartime poster for Westinghouse Electric Corporation to boost morale among women workers. It featured "Rosie the Riveter," a fictional figure introduced the previous year in a popular US song, with the speech bubble "We Can Do It!"

The poster was only used internally at Westinghouse Electric, but it was rediscovered in 1982 and reproduced in a *Washington Post Magazine* article. In the years that followed, it became an iconic image of female empowerment.

We've made one or two minor adjustments, but the message is as strong as ever!

We Can Do It!

MARK MY WORDS

How many words of four or more letters can you find on the board below?

M	I	C	H
E	L	L	E
L	A	V	A
U	G	H	N

Secret Service
Code Name Game

The US Secret Service uses code names for presidents and members of the First Family, as well as prominent figures, vehicles, and locations. The White House is known as "Castle" while Air Force One is "Angel" and Queen Elizabeth II is "Kittyhawk." Can you match the code names to the First Ladies and First Daughters from the clues opposite?

Edith Wilson (CLUE: It's all relative)	EVERGREEN
Mamie Eisenhower (CLUE: Paris)	TEMPO
Bess Truman (CLUE: Optimist)	RADIANCE
Eleanor Roosevelt (CLUE: Mars)	GRANDMA
Jacqueline Kennedy (CLUE: 13th anniversary)	RENAISSANCE
Pat Nixon (CLUE: Celestial)	ROSEBUD
Betty Ford (CLUE: Gilbert and Sullivan)	SUNNYSIDE
Rosalynn Carter (CLUE: Reindeer)	MARVEL
Nancy Reagan (CLUE: Arc)	MUSE
Barbara Bush (CLUE: Moon)	RAINBOW
Hillary Clinton (CLUE: Forever young)	LACE
Laura Bush (CLUE: Correct speed)	DANCER
Michelle Obama (CLUE: Florence)	SPRINGTIME
Melania Trump (CLUE: Melpomene)	PINAFORE
Chelsea Clinton (CLUE: Power)	RAINDANCE
Jenna Bush (CLUE: Nursery rhyme)	STARLIGHT
Malia Obama (CLUE: Shine)	TRANQUILITY
Sasha Obama (CLUE: Sled)	ROVER
Maria Shields Robinson (CLUE: Film festival)	TWINKLE
Ivanka Trump (CLUE: Venom)	ENERGY

MAJOR EVENTS TIMELINE

August 4, 1961 Barack Hussein Obama II is born to Ann Dunham and Barack Obama Sr. in Honolulu, Hawaii.

January 17, 1964 Michelle LaVaughn Robinson is born to Marian Shields and Fraser Robinson III in Chicago, Illinois.

May 1983 Barack graduates from Columbia University, New York.

May 1985 Michelle graduates from Princeton.

May 1988 Michelle graduates from Harvard Law School.

June 1989 25-year-old Michelle and 27-year-old Barack meet at law firm Sidley Austin and go on their first date.

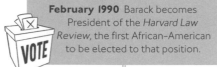

February 1990 Barack becomes President of the *Harvard Law Review*, the first African-American to be elected to that position.

May 1991 Barack graduates from Harvard Law School.

July 1991 Michelle leaves her position at Sidley Austin and becomes an assistant to the Mayor of Chicago, Richard M. Daley.

July 31, 1991 Barack proposes to Michelle at Gordon's restaurant in Chicago.

October 3, 1992 Barack Hussein Obama marries Michelle LaVaughn Robinson at Trinity United Church of Christ in South Chicago.

January 1993 Michelle becomes the Founding Director of nongovernmental organization Public Allies Chicago, which trains young people for jobs in community service.

June 1996 Michelle becomes associate dean of Student Services and the first director of Community Relations and Community Service at the University of Chicago.

September 5, 1996 Barack wins the race to become state senator of Illinois for the 13th district, with 82 per cent of the vote.

November 7, 1995 Barack's mother dies at the age of 52.

July 4, 1998 Malia Ann Obama is born at Chicago Medical Center.

November 7, 2000 Barack loses the election to become a congressman from Illinois to incumbent Bobby Rush.

June 10, 2001 Natasha (Sasha) born in Chicago Medical Center.

January 2002 Michelle begins working for University of Chicago Hospitals, as executive director for Community Affairs.

 November 2, 2004 Barack is elected US Senator with the largest victory margin for a state-wide race in the history of Illinois.

May 9, 2005 Michelle becomes vice president for Community and External Affairs at the University of Chicago Hospitals.

November 4, 2008 Barack wins the presidential election.

January 20, 2009 Barack inaugurated as the 44th President of the United States; Michelle is now the First Lady.

March 1, 2009 Michelle appears on the front cover of *Vogue*.

February 9, 2010 Michelle launches the campaign Let's Move! to reduce childhood obesity.

April 13, 2010 Michelle makes her first solo international trip, to Mexico.

April 2011 Michelle launches the campaign Joining Forces with Second Lady Jill Biden to support ex-servicemen and women.

May 29, 2012 Michelle's first book, *American Grown: The Story of the White House Kitchen Garden and Gardens Across America*, is published.

November 6, 2012 Barack is reelected for a second term.

May 2014 Michelle launches the campaign Reach Higher.

March 2015 Michelle launches the campaign Let Girls Learn.

January 13, 2017 Michelle gives her farewell remarks at the White House.

November 13, 2018 Michelle's memoir *Becoming* is published and breaks publishing records.

December 27, 2018 Michelle is named Most Admired Woman, knocking Hillary Clinton off the top spot for the first time in 17 years.

Courage

"You may not always have a comfortable life. And you will not always be able to solve all of the world's problems at once. But don't ever underestimate the impact you can have, because history has shown us that courage can be contagious, and hope can take on a life of its own."

KEYNOTE ADDRESS AT YOUNG AFRICAN WOMEN LEADERS FORUM, SOUTH AFRICA

"I'm thinking about girls like Malala. I'm thinking about those brave girls in Nigeria. I'm thinking about all the girls who will never make the headlines, who walk hours to school each day, who study late into the night because they are so hungry to fill every last bit of their God-given potential. If we can show just a tiny fraction of their courage and their commitment, then I know we can give all of our girls an education worthy of their promise."

UN GENERAL ASSEMBLY, SEPTEMBER 25, 2014

"Every day, you have the power to choose our better history—by opening your hearts and minds, by speaking up for what you know is right, by sharing the lessons of *Brown v. Board of Education*, the lessons you all learned right here in Topeka—wherever you go for the rest of your lives."

2014 TOPEKA HIGH SCHOOL COMMENCEMENT SPEECH, KANSAS

"Let's be very clear: Strong men—men who are truly role models—don't need to put down women to make themselves feel powerful. People who are truly strong lift others up. People who are truly powerful bring others together."

CAMPAIGN RALLY FOR HILLARY CLINTON, OCTOBER 14, 2016

Firsts for the Obamas

- Michelle was the first First Lady to attend an Ivy League university for her undergraduate degree.

- She was also the first First Lady to announce the winner of an Oscar. (At the 85th Academy Awards in 2013, she presented the Best Picture Oscar for *Argo*.)

- Barack Obama was the first president to hire a man to serve as White House Social Secretary (Jeremy Bernard, 2011–15). He also hired the first openly transgender staff member (Raffi Freedman-Gurspan, appointed as Outreach and Recruitment Director).

- Barack was the first president born outside of the forty-eight contiguous states (in Hawaii).

Barack Obama was also the first president to:

- Publicly endorse same-sex marriage.

- Appoint a former First Lady to the cabinet (Hillary Clinton).

- Appoint a Latino-American to the Supreme Court (Sonia Sotomayor) and first to appoint multiple women to the Supreme Court (Elena Kagan).

- Visit a federal prison (El Reno, Oklahoma).

- Publish a scientific paper while in office ("The Irreversible Momentum of Clean Energy," published in *Science*, January 9, 2019).

- Visit Myanmar, Cambodia, Laos, Kenya, and Ethiopia.

- Visit both a mosque and a synagogue while in office.

MOST ADMIRED PEOPLE 2018

American management consultancy firm Gallup has run an annual survey of the American public since 1946 posing the question: *What man and woman living today in any part of the world, do you admire most?*

In 1946, five-star general Douglas MacArthur claimed the prize. The Most Admired Woman category was added in 1948, with Eleanor Roosevelt emerging victorious. The Obamas reigned supreme in 2018, with Michelle winning for the first time. Barack has come out on top for the past 11 years, but she'll catch him before too long…

MOST ADMIRED WOMAN

1	Michelle Obama	15%
2	Oprah Winfrey (31st appearance on the list)	5%
3	Hillary Clinton (27th appearance)	4%
4	Melania Trump	4%
5	Queen Elizabeth II (record 50th appearance)	2%
6	Angela Merkel	2%
7	Ruth Bader Ginsburg	2%
8	Ellen DeGeneres	2%
9	Nikki Haley	1%
10	Malala Yousafzai	1%

MOST ADMIRED MAN

1	Barack Obama	19%
2	Donald Trump	13%
3	George W. Bush	2%
4	Pope Francis	2%
5	Bill Gates	1%
6	Bernie Sanders	1%
7	Bill Clinton (26th appearance)	1%
8	Dalai Lama	1%
9	Joe Biden	1%
10	Elon Musk	1%

THE OBAMAS: A Love Story

This chart shows the places around the US that Barack and Michelle lived. They just missed each other at Harvard Law School, with Michelle graduating in the summer of 1988 before Barack arrived in the autumn.

Finally, the stars aligned, and they met in the summer of 1989 in Chicago.

★ BARACK ★

Honolulu, Hawaii, 1961
Seattle, Washington, 1961
Honolulu, Hawaii, 1971
Los Angeles, California, 1979
New York City, New York, 1981
Chicago, Illinois, 1985
Cambridge, Massachusetts, fall 1988
Chicago, Illinois, summer 1989
Cambridge, Massachusetts, fall 1989
Chicago, Illinois, summer 1990
Cambridge, Massachusetts, fall 1990
Chicago, Illinois, 1991
Washington, DC, 2009

✶ MICHELLE ✶

Chicago, Illinois, 1964
Princeton, New Jersey, 1981
Cambridge, Massachusetts, 1985
Chicago, Illinois, summer 1988
Washington, DC, 2009

1 Washington	**6** Montana	**11** Alaska	**16** Colorado	**21** Iowa
2 Oregon	**7** Wyoming	**12** Hawaii	**17** Kansas	**22** Missouri
3 California	**8** Utah	**13** North Dakota	**18** Oklahoma	**23** Arkansas
4 Nevada	**9** Arizona	**14** South Dakota	**19** Texas	**24** Louisiana
5 Idaho	**10** New Mexico	**15** Nebraska	**20** Minnesota	**25** Wisconsin

26 Illinois	**33** South Carolina	**40** Massachusetts	**47** Delaware
27 Indiana	**34** Florida	**41** Maine	**48** Maryland
28 Kentucky	**35** North Carolina	**42** New York	**49** Washington, DC
29 Tennessee	**36** Michigan	**43** Rhode Island	**50** Virginia
30 Mississippi	**37** Ohio	**44** Connecticut	**51** West Virginia
31 Alabama	**38** New Hampshire	**45** Pennsylvania	
32 Georgia	**39** Vermont	**46** New Jersey	

School

- Michelle never liked eggs for breakfast, but her mom insisted on them as a source of protein. Michelle looked up the amount of protein in peanut butter and asked why it couldn't count as protein. After some debate, her mom changed her mind. And so, for the next nine years, Michelle had a peanut butter and jelly sandwich every day!

- Shortly after being given a new bike, Craig was picked up by a policeman for stealing it. The African American policeman refused to believe that a young black boy could innocently own a new bike. The officer ended up with a "brutal tongue-lashing" from their mom, who made him apologize to Craig.

- Craig became one of the best basketball players in Chicago and ended up at Mount Carmel—a private Catholic school—before winning a scholarship to Princeton. Craig became a starter on the Princeton basketball team in his second year, and his dad would drive for twelve hours across four states to watch his games.

- Michelle passed a test for the newly created Whitney M. Young Magnet High School, which drew in high-performing students from all races and backgrounds. Michelle needed to be up at 5 a.m. each day for the 90-minute bus journey.

- Michelle's first trip abroad was a school trip to Paris. She didn't even tell her parents it had been suggested because she thought it would cost far too much.

- Michelle was allowed to skip second grade after her mother Marian intervened. Marian had spent weeks lobbying after hearing her daughter tell her about the "hellish" environment in which the teacher had lost control of the class. After taking some tests, Michelle and other high-performing kids moved up to third grade.

- Michelle made friends with classmate Santita Jackson, daughter of Reverend Jesse Jackson, the preacher and political leader who had worked closely with Martin Luther King Jr. She joined Santita at the Bud Billiken Day Parade—the largest African-American parade in the US—and ended up on the news, which her parents were watching at home.

- In her final year of high school, Michelle was on track to graduate in the top 10 percent of her class, had been elected treasurer of the senior class, and had been accepted into the National Honor Society, which recognizes outstanding students.

- Wanting to emulate Craig, Michelle selected Princeton as her first choice college, but the school counselor said something that still sticks in Michelle's mind: "I'm not sure that you're Princeton material." Undaunted, Michelle sought help from the assistant principal and neighbor Mr Smith, who knew her, had seen her strengths, and trusted her with his kids. He wrote her a recommendation letter.

- Rather than pretending to be something she wasn't in her college essay, Michelle wrote about her faith in her own story, her father's struggle with multiple sclerosis, and her family's inexperience with higher education. Six months later, she received her acceptance letter.

Let's Move!

"In the end, as First Lady, this isn't just a policy issue for me. This is a passion. This is my mission. I am determined to work with folks across this country to change the way a generation of kids thinks about food and nutrition."

In February 2010, Michelle announced the launch of a public health initiative called Let's Move! Its bold mission is to solve the problem of childhood obesity within a generation. Its five goals are:

1 Creating a healthy start for children

2 Empowering parents and caregivers

3 Providing healthy food in schools

4 Improving access to healthy, affordable foods

5 Increasing physical activity

Among its achievements so far, "Let's Move!" has:

- Transformed school food through the Healthy, Hunger-Free Kids Act, which improved school-meal nutrition standards for the first time in fifteen years and helped provide healthy meals at little or no cost to those that needed it.

- Announced the FDA's (Food and Drug Administration) up-to-date Nutrition Facts labels for packaged foods.

- Launched the Department of Agriculture's MyPlate icon featuring each of the five food groups to help people make healthier choices.

- Introduced "Let's Move!" Salad Bars to schools, providing three million students with a salad bar.

- Begun Let's Move! Active Schools so parents can identify schools that seek to make 60 minutes of daily physical activity every day the norm for kids ages 6–17.

- Partnered with the US Olympic Committee to provide beginner athletic programs for low or no cost to more than two million children in 2016.

Women's Rights

"The women we honor today teach us three very important lessons. One, that as women, we must stand up for ourselves. The second, as women, we must stand up for each other. And finally, as women, we must stand up for justice for all."

SPEECH AT THE STATE DEPARTMENT WOMEN OF COURAGE AWARDS, 2009

"I am an example of what is possible when girls from the very beginning of their lives are loved and nurtured by people around them."

G20 SUMMIT, LONDON, 2009

"Women and girls can do whatever they want. There is no limit to what we as women can accomplish."

SPEECH ABOUT FUTURE FEMALE PRESIDENTS, 2012

"If you see another girl alone or isolated, you never know what they're going through. Keep that part of your heart open to each other. That's one thing we can do better as women— we can take better care of each other."

VISIT TO ELIZABETH GARRETT ANDERSON SCHOOL, LONDON, UK, 2011

"No country can ever truly flourish if it stifles the potential of its women and deprives itself of the contributions of half its citizens."

MANDELA WASHINGTON FELLOWSHIP, 2014

"The difference between a broken community and a thriving one is the presence of women who are valued."

WOMEN OF COURAGE AWARDS, 2009

The first inaugural ball to celebrate the commencement of a new presidential term was held one week after George Washington's election in 1789, in New York. George and Martha danced a minuet, in case you were wondering. It wasn't until 1809 that friends of the fourth president, James Madison, actually put on an official ball. This was held at Long's Hotel in Washington, DC and cost $4 a ticket for the 400 guests.

The Inaugural Balls for the most recent four presidents are depicted below along with judges' scores for each based on: (a) how much the couple actually seem to like each other; (b) their dance moves; and (c) their outfits.

TRUMPS (2017)

COST: **$90–100 million**

NUMBER OF OFFICIAL BALLS: **3**

MAIN PERFOMER: **Erin Boehme**

SCORES: **1, 3, 8**

OBAMAS (2009)

COST: **$53 million**
NUMBER OF OFFICIAL BALLS: **10**
MAIN PERFOMER: **Beyoncé**
SCORES: **10, 9, 9**

BUSHES (2001)

COST: **$30 million**
NUMBER OF OFFICIAL BALLS: **8**
MAIN PERFOMER: **Ricky Martin**
SCORES: **8, 2, 8**

CLINTONS (1993)

COST: **$29 million**
NUMBER OF OFFICIAL BALLS: **14**
MAIN PERFOMER: **Aretha Franklin**
SCORES: **8, 7, 9**

Dot-to-dot Michelle

Join the dots to locate Michelle in her rightful place, when she finally decides to save us all and run for president.

WORD CLOUD

MICHELLE'S SPEECH TO THE DEMOCRATIC NATIONAL CONVENTION IN 2008

On August 25, 2008, Michelle delivered the keynote address of the Democratic National Convention. It was her first national speech, which she used to reiterate that Barack shares Americans' beliefs, values, and dreams of a better future. Her speech was widely regarded as a huge success. In June 2008, Michelle's approval figures had been 48 percent, and by March 2009 they had skyrocketed to 72 percent.

DESIGN MICHELLE'S PRESIDENTIAL SEAL

The first known work on the Presidential Seal design was undertaken during the presidency of Millard Fillmore (in office 1850–1853.) President Fillmore sketched an eagle holding an olive branch and three arrows. The current design dates from 1945, but we thought it could use a little creative alteration to suit the needs of President Michelle Obama.

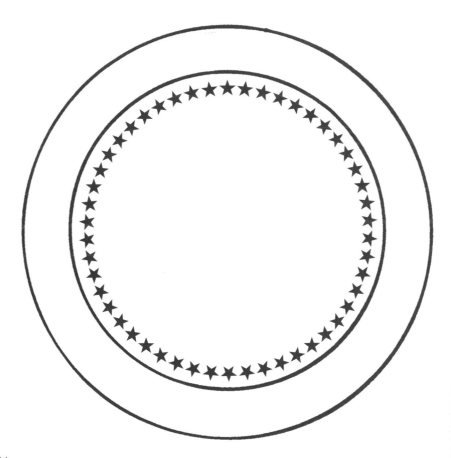

Success and Failure

"One of the lessons that I grew up with was to always stay true to yourself and never let what somebody says distract you from your goals."

INTERVIEW IN *MARIE CLAIRE*, 2008

"Whether you come from a council estate [public housing] or a country estate, your success will be determined by your own confidence and fortitude."

G20 SUMMIT, LONDON, 2009

"Success isn't about how much money you make, it's about the difference you make in people's lives."

DEMOCRATIC NATIONAL CONVENTION, 2012

"You should never view your challenges as a disadvantage. Instead, it's important for you to understand that your experience facing and overcoming adversity is actually one of your biggest advantages."

THE CITY COLLEGE OF NEW YORK'S COMMENCEMENT CEREMONY, 2016

"Failing is a crucial part of success. Every time you fail and get back up, you practice perseverance, which is the key to life. Your strength comes in your ability to recover."

THE WHITE HOUSE STUDENT WORKSHOP, WASHINGTON, DC, 2015

"Just try new things. Don't be afraid. Step out of your comfort zones and soar."

HOWARD UNIVERSITY, 2016

50th Birthday ✦

★ Michelle turned fifty on January 17, 2014, and Barack held a star-studded bash for her at the White House the following Saturday. Just like any other birthday party, Beyoncé performed, and John Legend sang two versions of "Happy Birthday."

The event hit the headlines for the leaked contents of the invitation, which asked guests to eat beforehand (outrageous!,) advising them to expect "Snacks & Sips & Dancing & Dessert." They were also told to "wear comfortable shoes…and practice your dance moves" for the evening's festivities, but all mobile phones were confiscated at the door, so few pictures emerged.

"At 2 a.m., there were the President and First Lady on the dance floor with a circle around them … It was Beyoncé and some of her dancers and the Obamas were more than keeping up. It looked like they got briefed on all the new moves. The First Lady danced like she was one of her daughters' generation."

AN UNNAMED GUEST TALKING TO PEOPLE.COM

Although the 500-strong guest list was kept a secret, it included:

Angela Bassett	Jennifer Hudson	Paul McCartney	James Taylor
Ashley Judd	John Legend	Smokey Robinson	Nancy Pelosi
Beyoncé	Magic Johnson	Stevie Wonder	Samuel. Jackson
Billie Jean King	Mary J. Blige	Hillary Clinton	Janelle Monae
Gladys Knight	Michael Jordan	Bill Clinton	

WHERE'S MICHELLE?

Can you spot our heroine (in miniature) among the contents of this famous office?

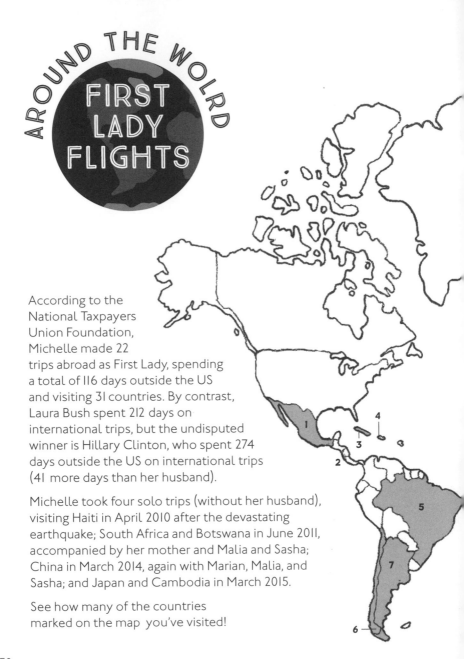

AROUND THE WOLRD
FIRST LADY FLIGHTS

According to the National Taxpayers Union Foundation, Michelle made 22 trips abroad as First Lady, spending a total of 116 days outside the US and visiting 31 countries. By contrast, Laura Bush spent 212 days on international trips, but the undisputed winner is Hillary Clinton, who spent 274 days outside the US on international trips (41 more days than her husband).

Michelle took four solo trips (without her husband), visiting Haiti in April 2010 after the devastating earthquake; South Africa and Botswana in June 2011, accompanied by her mother and Malia and Sasha; China in March 2014, again with Marian, Malia, and Sasha; and Japan and Cambodia in March 2015.

See how many of the countries marked on the map you've visited!

1 MEXICO
2 EL SALVADOR
3 CUBA
4 HAITI
5 BRAZIL
6 CHILE
7 ARGENTINA

8 IRELAND
9 UK
10 FRANCE
11 SPAIN
12 ITALY
13 GERMANY
14 DENMARK

15 NORWAY
16 MOROCCO
17 SENEGAL
18 LIBERIA
19 GHANA
20 TANZANIA
21 BOTSWANA

22 SOUTH
   AFRICA
23 JORDAN
24 SAUDI
   ARABIA
25 QATAR
26 RUSSIA

27 INDIA
28 CHINA
29 CAMBODIA
30 INDONESIA
31 JAPAN

THE OBAMAS: A Love Story

In the summer of 1989, Michelle was working as a lawyer in her first year at Chicago law firm Sidley Austin. And she was working her behind off, racking up 70 hours a week, most of which was spent alone at her desk (a lovely buffed walnut desk with a leather chair.)

And then her boss assigned her a summer associate. Enter Barack Obama, who, rumor had it, was the most gifted law student his professor at Harvard had ever seen.

The two of them met in the reception area at Michelle's forty-seventh-floor office. Barack didn't exactly make the finest impression, arriving late (one of Michelle's big no-nos) and damp from the rain, which he attempted to cover by grinning sheepishly and apologizing profusely.

Nevertheless, the pair established a rapport straight away, and with their free-flowing banter, they soon became friends over a meal at a fancy restaurant paid for by the company's dollar.

However, any potential romantic interest at the outset from Michelle's side was snuffed out by:

(a) recently swearing not to date
(b) the deal-breaker: Barack lighting up a cigarette after their first lunch

And then, one afternoon, as the two of them were finishing a meal, Barack confidently announced that he thought they should go out.

Cue feigned shock from Michelle, followed by a hurried, stern reminder of her recent no-dating policy and the fact that she was his adviser…

But not my boss, came the answer from Barack.

Education

"When you've worked hard and done well and walked through that doorway of opportunity, you do not slam it shut behind you. You reach back, and you give other folks the same chances that helped you succeed."

DEMOCRATIC NATIONAL CONVENTION, 2012

"I never cut class. I loved getting As, I liked being smart. I liked being on time. I thought being smart was cooler than anything in the world."

G20 SUMMIT, LONDON, 2009

"Education is the single most important civil rights issue that we face today."

BLACK HISTORY MONTH PANEL DISCUSSION, 2015

"The ability to read, write and analyze; the confidence to stand up and demand justice and equality; the qualifications and connections to get your foot in that door and take your seat at that table—all of that starts with education."

LET GIRLS LEARN EVENT, WASHINGTON, DC, 2016

"[Girls] know that education is their only path to self-sufficiency. It is their only chance to shape their own fate rather than have the limits of their lives dictated to them by others."

LET GIRLS LEARN EVENT, WASHINGTON, DC, 2016

"When girls are educated, their countries become stronger and more prosperous."

TRAVEL JOURNEY ENTRY ON A VISIT TO A SCHOOL IN DAKAR, SENEGAL, 2013

WHICH FIRST LADY? QUIZ

See if you can answer these brainteasers.

1 *Dear Socks, Dear Buddy* is a children's book about two presidential pets, but which First Lady wrote it?

A: Pat Nixon
B: Michelle Obama
C: Hillary Clinton
D: Nancy Reagan

2 Tricia and Julie were the daughters of which former First Lady?

A: Pat Nixon
B: Rosalynn Carter
C: Barbara Bush
D: Nancy Reagan

3 Which First Lady worked as a professional photographer for the *Washington Times-Herald* before meeting her husband-to-be in 1952?

A: Lady Bird Johnson
B: Betty Ford
C: Mamie Eisenhower
D: Jacqueline Kennedy

4 Which First Lady served as the first chair of the UN Commission on Human Rights and was crucially involved in the Universal Declaration of Human Rights?

A: Martha Washington
B: Edith Roosevelt
C: Eleanor Roosevelt
D: Edith Wilson

5 Who held the title of First Lady for the longest?

A: Eleanor Roosevelt
B: Martha Washington
C: Bess Truman
D: Laura Bush

6 Who was the first First Lady to be married to a divorced President?

A: Pat Nixon
B: Hillary Clinton
C: Jacqueline Kennedy
D: Nancy Reagan

7 Which First Lady won an Emmy Award for her television special *Tour of the White House*?

A: Pat Nixon
B: Hillary Clinton
C: Jacqueline Kennedy
D: Nancy Reagan

8 Which First Lady, who served for 5 years and 2 months, became a millionaire in her own right before her husband took office?

A: Lady Bird Johnson
B: Michelle Obama
C: Barbara Bush
D: Rosalynn Carter

9 Which First Lady was the first supposedly fluent in five languages?

A: Jacqueline Kennedy
B: Melania Trump
C: Rosalynn Carter
D: Nancy Reagan

10 Which First Lady had a mother-in-law who also served as a First Lady?

A: Betty Ford
B: Mary Todd Lincoln
C: Laura Bush
D: Barbara Bush

Embarrassing Mom

On February 13, 2019, after an unexpected yet hugely popular appearance at the Grammy Awards the previous night, Michelle received a priceless text from her mom, Marian, which led to the following exchange. Michelle posted it on her Twitter account with the Tweet:

When your mom doesn't think you're a "real" celebrity … Tonight in Phoenix, I shared this text thread from my mom from #Grammys night, and I just had to share it with all of you. #TextsFromMom

Mom >

Yesterday 5:10PM

I guess you were a hit at the Grammys 😊

I'm sitting here with Valerie and this text is so typically you

Did you watch it?!

I saw it because Gracie called me. Did you meet any of the real stars or did you run right after you were done

I told you I was going to be on it…

No you did not. I would have remembered that even though I don't remember much.

I thought I told you

And I Am A real star… by the way…

Yeah

MICHELLE'S MAJOR INITIATIVES

REACH HIGHER

On May 2, 2014, in San Antonio, Texas, Michelle launched her Reach Higher initiative to encourage students to complete their education past high school, whether it be via a professional training program or going on to college or university.

The US was previously the country with the highest percentage of people ages 24–34 years old with a college degree, but it had fallen to twelfth in 2010 with only 40 percent of 25- to 34-year-olds obtaining a degree.

The initiative raised awareness about applying for financial aid to attend college; launched a free texting service that offers personalized support on applying to college; and improved the school counselor program after studies showed that students meeting with school counselors were three times more likely to attend college and seven times more likely to apply for financial aid.

JOINING FORCES

Launched by Michelle and the Second Lady, Dr Jill Biden, in 2011, Joining Forces was an initiative to help raise awareness of the challenges that military families have to face. The pioneering initiative helped to provide employment opportunities for veterans and their spouses, offer assistance with the unique education requirements of their children, and provide access to wellness programs to help improve emotional and physical well-being.

On the fifth anniversary of the launch, Michelle announced that so far, more than 1.2 million veterans and military spouses had found work or training since 2011. In addition, forty companies pledged to hire more than 110,00 veterans in the period to 2021.

"For me, education has never been simply a policy issue— it's personal. Neither of my parents and hardly anyone in my neighborhood where I grew up went to college. But thanks to a lot of hard work and plenty of financial aid, I had the opportunity to attend some of the finest universities in this country."

LET GIRLS LEARN EVENT, WASHINGTON, DC, 2016

MICHELLE'S SPEECH AT THE MEMORIAL SERVICE FOR DR MAYA ANGELOU, JUNE 2014

In a moving memorial speech, Michelle Obama saluted "one of the greatest spirits our world has ever known" and thanked her for words which "carried a little black girl to the White House."

Princeton and Harvard

- In the summer of 1981, Michelle's dad drove her to Princeton along with Michelle's boyfriend David. They broke up that day.

- Craig was in his junior year at Princeton and one of the best players on the varsity basketball team. He lived in an upstairs bedroom at the Third World Center (TWC), an offshoot of the university dedicated to supporting students of color.

- Michelle's financial aid package at Princeton necessitated she get a job, which she secured at the TWC as assistant to the director, Czerny Brasuell. Czerny suggested that Michelle run an after-school program for kids of faculty members, and soon Michelle was looking after four children several afternoons a week.

- Unbeknown to Michelle, the mother of one of Michelle's two roommates in her first year at Princeton, a teacher from New Orleans, complained to the university that her daughter had been assigned a black roommate. Her daughter moved out into a single room shortly afterward, but Michelle didn't know why at the time.

- Michelle majored in sociology and minored in African-American studies. She graduated *cum laude* with a bachelor of arts degree in summer 1985. Her thesis was titled "Princeton-educated Blacks and the Black Community," which she dedicated to "Mom, Dad, Craig and all of my special friends: Thank you for loving me and always making me feel good about myself."

- Michelle's thesis advisor wrote her an underwhelming recommendation letter to go with her application to Harvard Law School. After she worked extremely hard on her thesis, the professor wrote another letter, this one full of praise, and was accepted to Harvard.

- Michelle entered Harvard Law School in September 1985. The following spring, she volunteered at the student-operated Harvard Legal Aid Bureau, a service provided free of charge to low-income clients. It involved working unpaid for up to 20 hours each week.

- At the end of her sophomore year at Harvard, Michelle was offered the position of summer associate at the Chicago offices of law firm Sidley Austin. She later joined the firm as an associate after graduating from Harvard in May 1988.

HONORS AND AWARDS

Michelle has been awarded six honorary degrees and five awards, four of which were presented jointly.

DOCTORATES

Honorary doctor of public service from George Washington University, May 16, 2010

Honorary doctor of laws from Spelman College, May 15, 2011

Honorary doctor of public health from Oregon State University, June 18, 2012

Honorary doctor of humane letters from The City College of New York, June 3, 2016

Honorary doctor of laws from Bowie State University, May 17, 2013

Honorary doctor of human letters from Jackson State University, April 23, 2016

AWARDS

National Education Association Human and Civil Rights Award, July 1, 2018

Freedom of the City of Cape Town, June 2013 (shared with Barack)

Jerald Washington Memorial Founders' Award by the National Coalition for Homeless Veterans (NCHV), April 27, 2012 (shared with Barack)

Jerald Washington Memorial Founders' Award by the National Coalition for Homeless Veterans, May 19, 2015 (shared with the Second Lady, Dr Jill Biden)

Freedom of Dublin City, February 2017 (shared with Barack)

"When someone is cruel or acts like a bully, you don't stoop to their level. No, our motto is, 'When they go low, we go high.'"

Michelle Obama offered this aspirational, dignified advice during a rousing speech at the 2016 Democratic National Convention amid a bruising run-up to the election. In the aftermath of this famous speech, author Philip Collins wrote: "Barack Obama may be the best male speaker in living memory …and the second-best speaker in his own family."

SPOT THE DIFFERENCE

Can you spot the seven differences between this scene of the Oval Office and the scene opposite?

WHERE'S MICHELLE?

Can you spot our heroine (in miniature) aboard this famous aircraft?

Same-sex Marriage

"Thousands of people were gathering in front of the White House at that time to celebrate, and my staff was calling me, everyone was celebrating, people were crying, and I thought, 'I want to be in that.' Also, we had worked to make sure that the White House was lit up in the LGBT colors. It was beautiful. We stood along with all the cheering crowd, off to the side, mind you, so no one would see us, with security surrounding us, and we tried to have our tender mother–daughter moment, but we just took it in. I held her tight, and my feeling was, we are moving forward. Change is happening."

ABOUT ESCAPING THE WHITE HOUSE TO CELEBRATE THE COURT RULING TO LEGALIZE SAME-SEX MARRIAGE

"This is an important issue for millions of Americans, and for Barack and me, it really comes down to the values of fairness and equality we want to pass down to our girls. These are basic values that kids learn at a very young age and that we encourage them to apply in all areas of their lives. And in a country where we teach our children that everyone is equal under the law, discriminating against same-sex couples just isn't right. It's as simple as that."

ON TWITTER LIVE Q+A, 2012

"...If proud Americans can be who they are and boldly stand at the altar with who they love ... then surely, surely we can give everyone in this country a fair chance at that great American Dream."

DEMOCRATIC NATIONAL CONVENTION, 2012

WHITE HOUSE WORD SEARCH

BECOMING
FIRST LADY
HARVARD
LAVAUGHN
MALIA

PRINCETON
ROBINSON
SASHA
SUNNY
WHITE HOUSE

```
N O S N I B O R A X N F J C N
G Y E W V F A T C W S R P B S
Q N G P S B A L U A P N N G L
Z N I W H I T E H O U S E A J
F S Q M L M V E K S Q E V G G
I P X A O Z R J W U U A I P C
F R M S U C Q W B A U N H B F
T I Y W Q G E H Q G I K N D A
I N R A W M M B H D F P S Y R
F C D S S L V N V R S A S H A
O E S D T X W A G A N H Z Z Z
F T N P M L U T G V T R G M C
V O U H R K A I C R F E F H R
Y N N S N I Y D S A U W Q E Y
B L Y M D H L E Y H R Y Q H S
```

Barack made his debut as a comic-book character in July 2007, when he appeared as a US Senator. Barack became president in January 2009. After Marvel learned that he had amassed quite a collection of *Spider-Man* and *Conan the Barbarian* comics, it decided to put him on the front cover of issue number 583 of *The Amazing Spider-Man* and feature him in the story *Spidey Meets the President*. The issue sold out in minutes.

However, it wasn't until April 2009 that Michelle was transformed into a comic-book superhero called *Female Force: Michelle Obama*. We've put together a new superhero for you to color in.

THE OBAMAS: A Love Story

Over the next few days following Barack's declaration, which Michelle had half-heartedly rebuffed, he proceeded, in a particularly lawyerly fashion, to prepare the case for the two of them going out.

ARGUMENTS FOR THE DEFENSE

(a) Mutual compatibility

(b) Shared sense of humor

(c) Availability

(d) A telling and immediate dismissal of anyone else they met

(e) The firm might welcome it, seeing as it would improve the odds of his committing to the firm!

Their first unofficial date was a company-organized outing to see *Les Misérables*, which they both agreed at the interval was horrible. So they snuck out, ducking and weaving past other senior members of the firm during their rapid exit.

They walked to a nearby bar, Barack shuffling along with his characteristic casualness, while Michelle adopted her equally characteristic rapid power walk. But this time, she made a conscious effort to slow down. She found herself caring about what he had to say, but held something back. She wasn't ready for someone to disrupt her well-ordered existence. Well, not yet, anyway.

A couple of days later, Barack asked if Michelle could give him a ride to a barbecue for summer associates. When some of his colleagues started playing basketball, Barack sauntered over to join them. Michelle noticed his easy rapport with everyone, along with his power, agility, and grace. As she drove him back, there was an undeniable tension in the air between them, but she second-guessed herself. Did he just see her as the reliable friend in the fancy and air-conditioned yet sensible Saab who would drive him around when called upon?

Waiting for each other to say goodbye first like a couple of nervous teenagers, Barack stepped up and popped the question. No, not that one. Like an old smoothie, he asked her if they should get some ice cream.

"I treated her to the finest ice cream Baskin-Robbins had to offer, our dinner table doubling as the curb. I kissed her, and it tasted like chocolate."

A plaque immortalizing Michelle and Barack's first kiss was created in 2012 by the owners of a nearby shopping center outside the site of the former ice-cream parlor in Chicago's Hyde Park neighborhood. Cute!

White House True or False?

1 The desk used by the President in the Oval Office was a gift from Queen Elizabeth II.

2 The President and the members of the First Family are not allowed to open any windows in the White House.

3 Barack Obama had the White House tennis court redesigned to double as a basketball court.

4 The First Family has to move into the White House within a twelve-hour period.

5 The Obamas were the only family in 100 years to send their children to a Washington, DC public school rather than a private one.

6 The President is not allowed to drive on a public road.

7 Queen Elizabeth II has met every US president since her reign began.

8 The White House has a permanent executive pastry chef.

9 Thomas Jefferson enjoyed ice cream so much that he had an ice house excavated on the White House grounds.

10 The presidential retreat Camp David was originally named Paradise.

11 Air Force One is a call sign used to describe any US Air Force aircraft carrying the President.

12 Donald Trump is the first president in over 130 years not to have a pet in the White House.

13 In 1994, a light plane crashed into the White House grounds.

14 George Washington never lived in the White House.

15 George W. Bush had a bowling alley installed in the basement of the White House.

16 The White House is the only private residence of a head of state that members of the public can visit for free.

17 The President does not have to pay for food consumed by his family and personal guests.

18 Margaret Thatcher claimed that she saw the ghost of Abraham Lincoln while she was staying at the White House.

19 There are 232 rooms in the White House.

20 President Woodrow Wilson kept forty-eight sheep on the lawn of the White House.

Escape the Social Event Maze

Michelle has to return to the White House for a function that former First Ladies are required to attend. Help her navigate her way out, avoiding the horrifying demons obstructing her path.

DESIGN YOUR OWN

MICHELLE OBAMA STAMP

Michelle was named the "Best Dressed Woman in the World" in 2013 by *The Sunday Times* in the UK and dubbed the "First Lady of Fashion." The newspaper's *Style* magazine later published a design for a postage stamp with Michelle replacing the Queen. It's time for you to flex your creative muscles and come up with a design fit for a queen.

1st

THE FIRST GRANNY

Michelle's mom, Marian Shields Robinson, moved into the White House in January 2009 to help instill a sense of normalcy in the lives of Malia and Sasha, who were then only ten and seven. Not wanting a lot of fuss or attention, people warmed to her instantly. Here are some of her funniest and sweetest comments.

"If I can't do it fast, I'm not doing it. You don't run just to be running— you run to win!"

Marian said this after she had taken a fall and withdrew from the National Senior Games (she used to compete regularly in the 50- and 100-yard dash at the Illinois Senior Games)

"You try to get your kids not to think in the same way you did when you were coming along because you pass down—I call them 'your issues'—you pass down your issues and, a lot of times, they don't apply to their time and their life. They will have their own issues; they don't need mine in their head."

ON PRUDENTLY KEEPING SOME OF HER OPINIONS TO HERSELF

"It makes it very easy to be a grandmother when your children are good parents."

ON ADJUSTING TO LIFE IN THE WHITE HOUSE

"I have candy, they stay up late—come to my house, they watch TV as long as they want to, we'll play games until the wee hours . . . I do everything that grandmothers do that they're not supposed to."

ON BEING A SUPER-COOL GRANDMOTHER!

"The White House reminds me of a museum, and it's like, how do you sleep in a museum?"

Marian asked this shortly after Michelle had persuaded her to move into the White House

"When I grow up, I would like to be like Michelle Obama."

Marian's answer to Gayle King's question about what makes her most proud about her daughter

"I talked them into allowing me to do my own laundry."

On not letting living in the White House go to her head. She taught Malia and Sasha how to do their own laundry to boot

NAME THAT SONG

For Michelle's *Becoming book* tour, American musician Questlove put together a Spotify playlist called "The Michelle Obama Musiaqualogy," featuring more than 300 tracks split into three volumes. See if you can guess the songs below from the emoji picture clues.

SIX DEGREES OF KEVIN BACON

If you're not familiar with this game, then you should be because it's fun (if you get it right) and face-contortingly infuriating if you don't.

The idea is to link two people through the various films or TV shows they've been in. For example, to link Tom Hanks and Judi Dench would take just two moves: Tom Hanks was in *Road to Perdition* with Daniel Craig; Daniel Craig was in *Casino Royale* with Judi Dench. The name is a take on the game Six Degrees of Separation and named after Kevin Bacon because, well, he's basically been in every film ever.

Can you link Michelle Obama to Christopher Walken in three moves? We're giving you part of the first link (Michelle appeared in a cameo in the season-six finale of US TV show *Parks and Recreation*). And when you're done with that, try linking Michelle Obama with Joseph Gordon-Levitt.

	PERSON	FILM / TV SHOW
1		*Parks and Recreation*
2		
3	Christopher Walken	

	PERSON	FILM / TV SHOW
1		*Parks and Recreation*
2		
3	Joseph Gordon-Levitt	

Write a Rude Message to Trump

Michelle has two minutes to leave the White House before the next president arrives. She comes up with the perfect idea for a childish prank. Leave a rude message for Donald Trump in the famous Resolute desk that only he will find! Write it with your non-writing hand, and he'll never know it was you. Just don't sign it with your name at the bottom.

COLOR-IN RAINBOW WHITE HOUSE

After the landmark Supreme Court ruling on June 26, 2015, to allow same-sex couples to marry across the US, a few days later the White House was illuminated with rainbow colors for the evening to celebrate the change. The following day, President Obama said:

"I didn't have the chance to comment on how good the White House looked in rainbow colors ... to see people gathered in the evening on a beautiful summer night and to feel whole and to feel accepted and to feel they had a right to love, that was pretty cool. That was a good thing."

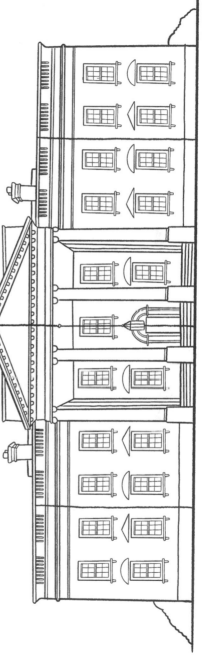

FIRST LADY OF FASHION

As soon as Michelle became First Lady, interest in her wardrobe became feverish. Everything she chose to put on became the source of public debate, but one thing is beyond doubt: By the end of her tenure as First Lady, Michelle was a fashion icon.

Here are two of Michelle's iconic dresses, but we need you to apply the color!

Michelle wore this Tracy Reese dress at the 50th anniversary of Dr. Martin Luther King's "I Have a Dream" speech in 2013.

Michelle wore this
Alice & Olivia skirt
and top combo when
visiting Siem Reap,
Cambodia, in 2015.

MARK MY WORDS

How many words of six or more letters can you find on the board below?

F	I	R	S
T	L	A	D
Y	O	F	T
H	E	U	S

DREAM DINNER PARTY GUEST LIST

You can invite any six people alive today to join you for a dinner party. Who would you choose?

I'd go for Michelle, Barack, David Attenborough, J. K. Rowling, Stephen Fry, and Elon Musk. Choose wisely!

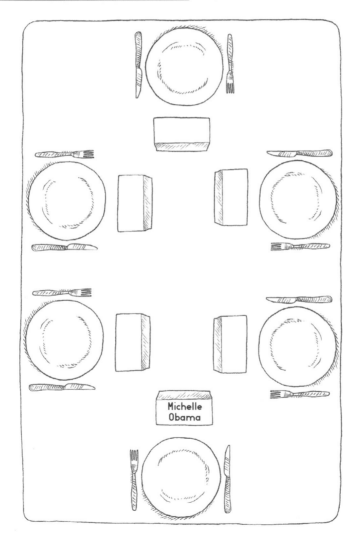

Michelle Obama

PRESIDENTIAL MEDAL OF FREEDOM WINNERS

President Barack H. Obama awarded the Presidential Medal of Freedom—the highest civilian honor in the United States—to the following people during his tenure as 44th President of the US.

* awarded posthumously

AUGUST 12, 2009

Nancy Goodman Brinker (founder of the largest breast cancer charity in the US)

Dr. Pedro José Greer, Jr. (physician, philanthropist, and founder of an agency providing medical care to the homeless)

Stephen Hawking (theoretical physicist, cosmologist, and author)

Representative Jack Kemp* (former professional quarterback, long-serving member of the House of Representatives and former Housing Secretary)

Senator Edward Kennedy (long-serving senator from Massachusetts)

Billie Jean King (legendary tennis player)

Reverend Joseph Lowery (minister and leader in the Civil Rights movement)

Joseph Medicine Crow (Native American tribal chief, author, and historian)

Harvey Milk* (gay rights activist and politician)

Justice Sandra Day O'Connor (retired associate justice of the Supreme Court)

Sidney Poitier (Academy Award-winning actor, director, and diplomat)

Chita Rivera (actress, singer, and dancer)

Mary Robinson (former President of Ireland)

Dr. Janet Davison Rowley (human geneticist and cancer specialist)

Archbishop Desmond Tutu (South African Anglican cleric, anti-Apartheid campaigner and human rights activist)

Muhammad Yunus (Bangladeshi social entrepreneur and Nobel Peace Prize winner)

FEBRUARY 15, 2011

John H. Adams (founder of the National Resources Defense Council)

Maya Angelou (poet, writer, and civil rights activist)

Warren Buffett (business magnate and philanthropist)

President George H.W. Bush (the 41st president of the US)

Jasper Johns (painter, sculptor, and printmaker)

Gerda Weissmann Klein (Academy Award-winning writer and human rights activist)

Representative John Lewis (politician and civil rights leader)

Dr. Tom Little* (optometrist and leader of the International Assistance Mission in Afghanistan who was killed in the 2010 Badakhshan massacre)

Yo-Yo Ma (Chinese-American cellist)

Sylvia Mendez (civil rights activist)

Angela Merkel (long-serving Chancellor of Germany)

Stan Musial (baseball legend)

Bill Russell (basketball legend)

Jean Kennedy Smith (former US Ambassador to Ireland)

John J. Sweeney (former President of the American Federation of Labor and Congress of Industrial Organizations)

JUNE 30, 2011

Robert M. Gates (former secretary of defense and director of central intelligence)

MAY 29, 2012

Madeleine Albright (former secretary of state and ambassador to the UN)

John Doar (lawyer and former Deputy assistant attorney-general for civil rights)

Bob Dylan (legendary, multi award-winning singer–songwriter)

Dr. William Foege (epidemiologist who played a critical role in the eradication of smallpox)

John Glenn (fighter pilot, astronaut, engineer, and politician)

Gordon Hirabayashi (sociologist who fought against Japanese-American internment in World War II)

Dolores Huerta (labor leader and civil rights activist)

Jan Karski* (Polish soldier and activist)

Juliette Gordon Low (founder of the Girl Scouts)

Toni Morrison (Pulitzer Prize-winning novelist and academic)

Justice John Paul Stevens (lawyer and former associate justice of the US Supreme Court)

Pat Summitt (former US basketball player and coach)

JUNE 13, 2012

Shimon Peres (former Israeli President and Prime Minister)

NOVEMBER 20, 2013

Ernie Banks (baseball legend)

Ben Bradlee (executive editor of The Washington Post who published the Pentagon Papers and the stories documenting Watergate)

Bill Clinton (the 42nd president of the US)

Senator Daniel Inouye* (long-serving senator from Hawaii and World War II Medal of Honor winner)

Daniel Kahneman (Nobel Prize–winning psychologist and economist)

Senator Richard Lugar (long-serving senator from Indiana)

Loretta Lynn (country music singer-songwriter)

Mario Molina (chemist known for his role in the discovery of the Antarctic ozone hole)

Sally Ride* (astronaut who became the first American woman in space)

Bayard Rustin* (civil rights and gay rights activist)

Arturo Sandoval (jazz trumpeter, pianist, and composer)

Dean Smith (basketball coaching legend)

Gloria Steinem (journalist, social political activist, and spokesperson for the feminist movement)

Cordy Tindell "C.T." Vivian (minister and civil rights leader)

Patricia Wald (judge and first woman appointed to the District of Columbia circuit, where she served as chief judge)

Oprah Winfrey (talk show host, producer, media executive and philanthropist)

NOVEMBER 24, 2014

Alvin Ailey* (choreographer and activist)

Isabel Allende (Chilean writer)

Tom Brokaw (journalist and author)

James Chaney* (civil rights worker murdered by the KKK in 1964)

Mildred Dresselhaus (pioneering multi-award-winning physicist)

Representative John Dingell (longest-ever serving congressperson in American history)

Andrew Goodman* (civil rights worker murdered by the KKK in 1964)

Ethel Kennedy (civil rights campaigner)

Suzan Harjo (Native American rights activist)

Representative Abner Mikva (politician, judge and White House Counsel)

Representative Patsy Takemoto Mink* (long-serving senator from Hawaii)

Representative Edward Roybal (long-serving congressman from California)

Michael Schwerner* (civil rights worker murdered by the KKK in 1964)

Charles Sifford (professional golfer and first African American to play on the PGA Tour)

Robert Solow (Nobel Prize-winning economist)

Meryl Streep (actress who has been nominated for a record twenty-one Academy Awards, winning three)

Marlo Thomas (actress, producer and author)

Stevie Wonder (legendary singer-songwriter and winner of twenty-five Grammy awards)

NOVEMBER 24, 2015

Yogi Berra (baseball legend)

Bonnie Carroll (military veteran and founder of the Tragedy Assistance Program for Survivors)

Representative Shirley Chisholm* (politician who became the first African American woman elected to Congress)

Emilio Estefan (multi-award-winning musician and producer)

Gloria Estefan (award-winning singer, songwriter, actress, and businesswoman)

Billy Frank, Jr.* (Native American environmental leader)

Representative Lee Hamilton (long-serving congressman from Indiana)

Katherine G. Johnson (mathematician and NASA employee critical to the success of the first manned US spaceflights)

Willie Mays (baseball legend)

Senator Barbara Mikulski (long-serving congressman from Maryland)

Itzhak Perlman (violinist and conductor)

William Ruckelshaus (first head of the Environmental Protection Agency)

Stephen Sondheim (multi-award-winning composer and lyricist)

Steven Spielberg (film director, producer and two-time Best Director at the Academy Awards)

Barbra Streisand (multi-award-winning singer, actress and filmmaker)

James Taylor (award-winning singer–songwriter and guitarist)

Minoru Yasui (lawyer advocating for Japanese-American rights during World War II)

NOVEMBER 22, 2016

Kareem Abdul-Jabbar (legendary basketball player)

Elouise Cobell* (Native American tribal elder and activist)

Ellen DeGeneres (multi-award-winning television host, acress, writer and human rights activist)

Robert De Niro (multi-award-winning actor, producer and director)

Richard Garwin (physicist and designer of the hydrogen bomb)

Bill Gates (principal founder of Microsoft Corporation and philanthropist)

Melinda Gates (former general manager of Microsoft and philanthropist)

Frank Gehry (contemporary architect)

Margaret H. Hamilton (computer scientist and systems engineer)

Tom Hanks (actor, filmmaker and two-time Best Actor at the Academy Awards)

Grace Hopper* (computer scientist and US Navy Rear Admiral)

Michael Jordan (legendary basketball player described by the NBA as the "greatest basketball player of all time")

Maya Lin (designer, architect, and artist)

Lorne Michaels (TV producer and actor who created Saturday Night Live)

Newt Minow (lawyer and former chair of the Federal Communications Commission)

Eduardo Padrón (president of Miami Dade College)

Robert Redford (actor, director, and founder of Sundance Film Festival)

Diana Ross (former lead singer of The Supremes and later solo artist, actress, and producer)

Vin Scully (legendary baseball sportscaster)

Bruce Springsteen (multi-award-winning singer–songwriter)

Cicely Tyson (multi-award-winning actress)

JANUARY 12, 2017

Joseph R. Biden, Jr. (former US vice president)

OBAMA
CROSSWORD

ACROSS

3 In 1996, Barack was elected senator of which state?

5 Which female singer performed at Michelle's 50th birthday?

6 Which country did Michelle visit on her first solo trip as First Lady?

7 Which member of the British Royal Family did Michelle jointly launch the Invictus Games with in 2015?

8 Michelle's brother Craig is associated with which sport?

11 What was the name of Michelle's first book, published in 2012 about the history of the White House Kitchen Garden?

DOWN

1 Which town in Alabama did Michelle visit in March 2015 to commemorate the 50th anniversary of three famous protest marches?

2 Which Spike Lee film did Barack and Michelle watch on their first date?

4 What was Michelle's father's first name?

9 Which film did Michelle present an Oscar to at the Academy Awards in 2013?

10 Which famous magazine did Michelle appear on the cover for in March 2009?

12 Which European capital city did Malia Obama spend a summer working in as an intern at the US Embassy?

Kids' State Dinner Menu

Michelle hosted five kids' state dinners at the White House, from 2012 to 2016. Children from each state (along with Washington, DC, American Samoa, Guam and the Northern Mariana Islands) were asked to send in healthy lunchtime recipe submissions and the winners from each state or territory would be invited to the White House along with their families.

Several of the winning recipes were served for the state dinner. We're fans of the 2015 menu (mainly for the pun-based main course).

For the 2014 kids' state dinner, the President made an appearance and cheekily let slip his family's nutritional weaknesses:

"Malia, ice cream. I mean, basically, it's very hard for her to turn down ice cream. Sasha ... She pretty much takes dessert whenever she can. Pie. She's like me. My big thing: chips and guacamole ... And the first lady: French fries!"

Mediterranean Rockin' Roasted Vegetables in Cool Cucumber Boats
(Wisconsin)

Vegetable Confetti Spring Rolls
(Washington, DC)

California Rainbow Taco, Mic–Kale Obama Slaw and Barack–amole
(California)

Oodles of Zoodles and Avocado Pistachio Pesto
(Arizona)

Aloha Sorbet
(Hawaii)

Mary's Garden's Smoothie
(Iowa)

Michelle's Favorite
CHILDREN'S
BOOKS

Over the years, Michelle has revealed her favorite children's books.

Alexander and the Terrible, Horrible, No Good, Very Bad Day
by Judith Viorst
(Michelle read this in 2009 to a group of Washington, DC, elementary school children)

Babar by Jean de Brunhoff
(One of the first books she took out of her local library in Chicago)

Brown Bear, Brown Bear, What Do You See? by Bill Martin Jr.
(Michelle read this book—most of it without having to look at the words!—at a
community health organization in Washington, DC, to a thrilled audience)

The Cat in the Hat by Dr Seuss
(Michelle says, "I know every word of every Dr Seuss, anything, still by heart.")

Goodnight Moon by Margaret Wise Brown
(One of Michelle's favorite books to read to Malia and Sasha when they were growing up)

Olivia by Ian Falconer
(Michelle read this book in 2008 to a group of children at the University of
South Carolina's Children's Center)

Pippi Longstocking by Astrid Lindgren
(The first book Michelle fell in love with as a child; she said of it: "I was really fascinated
with this strong little girl that was the center of everything. And she was almost magical in
a way. I mean, she was stronger and tougher than anyone. She had superhuman strength.")

Where the Wild Things Are by Maurice Sendak
(Barack Obama said of this kids' classic: "My wife still thinks that I'm Max...
that I'm getting into mischief all the time.")

Michelle's Favorite BOOKS

Educated by Tara Westover
("It's an engrossing read, a fresh perspective on the power of an education,
and it's also a testament to the way grit and resilience can shape our lives.")

White Teeth by Zadie Smith
("I love the way the story weaves together so many complex and powerful forces that affect
our lives and our relationships—family and parenting, religion, and politics, and so much
more. Plus, it's just plain funny. I love books that make me laugh every now and then.")

Conversations with Myself by Nelson Mandela
("I like to flip through it from time to time because it always seems to
give me an extra boost when I need it.")

Song of Solomon by Toni Morrison

The Grapes of Wrath by John Steinbeck

Life of Pi by Yann Martel

An American Marriage by Tayari Jones

Exit West by Mohsin Hamid

Commonwealth by Ann Patchett

The Light of the World by Elizabeth Alexander

Biggest Book Deals of All Time

In May 2017, the Obamas signed a book deal worth $65 million for their autobiographies. It was the second biggest book deal in history, after prolific novelist James Patterson signed a deal in 2009 worth up to $150 million to write seventeen books over three years. Below are the ten biggest deals in history, not including Patterson's unique deal.

TITLE	AUTHOR	VALUE	DATE
Becoming (and Barack's unnamed autobiography)	Michelle Obama and Barack Obama	$65 million	2017
Fall of Giants, Winter of the World and *Edge of Eternity*	Ken Follett	$50 million ($57.5 million today)	2010
My Life	Bill Clinton	$15 million ($20 million today)	2004
Hard Choices	Hillary Clinton	$14 million ($14.8 million today)	2014
Crossing the Threshold of Hope	Pope John Paul II	$8.5 million ($14.4 million today)	1994
The Downing Street Years and *The Path to Power*	Margaret Thatcher	$4.6 million ($11.3 million today)	1993–95
Born to Run	Bruce Springsteen	$10 million ($10.5 million today)	2016
The Girl with the Lower Back Tattoo	Amy Schumer	$9 million ($9.5 million today)	2015
The Casual Vacancy	J.K. Rowling	$8 million ($8.75 million today)	2012
Life	Keith Richards	$7.3 million ($8.4 million today)	2010

INAUGURATION ATTENDEE QUIZ

Can you guess the following attendees of Barack's 2009 inauguration from the clues below?

1 The eldest of the living former Presidents of the United States.

2 The heroic captain of US Airways Flight 1549, which crash-landed in the Hudson River in New York.

3 Two-time Academy Award–winner for Best Actor, who was considered for the role of Michael Corleone in *The Godfather* but lost out to Al Pacino.

4 The 38th Governor (or should that be Governator) of California.

5 As of March 2019, this actor's films have achieved the highest total gross revenue.

6 Born Gordon Sumner, this seventeen-time Grammy Award-winner later changed his name to something with a bit more bite.

7 Actress and musician who shot to fame in Disney Channel's *Hannah Montana* in 2006.

8 Basketball legend well known for his rivalry with Larry Bird.

9 Film director, who directed the *Back to the Future* trilogy and *Forrest Gump*.

10 Long-serving Congressman and the only living speaker from the March on Washington, where Martin Luther King Jr. delivered his "I Have A Dream" speech.

FAMOUS MICHELLES QUIZ

1 Which band wrote the song "Michelle," some of which is sung in French?

2 Which Michelle famously gained emancipation from her parents, age fifteen, before making a name for herself in teen drama *Dawson's Creek*?

3 Which Michelle played the iconic character Catwoman in the 1992 film *Batman Returns*?

4 Which Michelle memorably played Yu Shu Lien in the 2000 classic film *Crouching Tiger, Hidden Dragon*?

5 Which Michelle played Lady Mary Crawley in *Downton Abbey*?

6 Which actress played the role Michelle Flaherty in the *American Pie* films?

7 Which Michelle appeared in the blockbuster film *The Fast and the Furious* and *Resident Evil*?

8 Which Michele was a candidate for the 2012 Republican Presidential nomination and became associated with the Tea Party movement?

9 Which Michelle became the youngest player to qualify for a United States Golf Association tournament, at just age 10?

10 Where would you find 1376 Michelle?
(CLUE: It was discovered in 1935.)

AN EPIC PLAYLIST FOR AN EPIC WOMAN

Questlove, the drummer and joint frontman for Grammy-Award-winning band The Roots, who serve as Jimmy Fallon's in-house band, curated a playlist for Michelle's *Becoming* tour. Apparently, it took him ten years to put together! His playlist is so cool that I haven't heard of most of the tracks. So here's a semi-cool playlist that I've curated in Michelle's honor. Obviously each time she plays one of them at an event, I'm claiming the credit.

***Flawless** Beyoncé featuring Chimamanda Ngozi Adichie

#1 Must Have Sleater-Kinney

9 to 5 Dolly Parton

ABC Jackson Five

Ain't That Good News Sam Cooke

Ain't Nobody Rufus and Chaka Khan

Ain't Nothin' Wrong KC and the Sunshine Band

Ain't No Mountain High Enough Marvin Gaye and Tammi Terrell

Ain't Nuthin' But a She Thing Salt-N-Pepa

Airmail Special Ella Fitzgerald

A Little Party Never Killed Nobody (All We Got) Fergie, Q-Tip, GoonRock

A Living Human Girl The Regrettes

All of Me John Legend

Alright Kendrick Lamar

American Woman Lenny Kravitz

Amigas Cheetahs The Cheetah Girls

Anaconda Nicki Minaj

And I Am Telling You I'm Not Going Jennifer Hudson

A Rose Is Still a Rose Aretha Franklin

As Stevie Wonder

At Last Etta James

A Woman's Worth Alicia Keys

Baby I Love You Aretha Franklin

Baby, I'm For Real The Originals

Baby Love The Supremes

Back up Train Al Green

Back To Basics The Barden Bellas (from the soundtrack to *Pitch Perfect 2*)

Bad Girls Donna Summer

Bad Girls M.I.A.

Bad Reputation Joan Jett

Be Thankful for What You Got William DeVaughn

Better Be Good to Me Tina Turner

Bewitched Ella Fitzgerald

Big Boss Theme Peter Thomas Sound Orchestra

Billie Jean Michael Jackson

Black Gold Esperanza Spalding, Algebra Blessett, Lionel Loueke

Blame It on the Boogie Jackson Five

Blue Moon Billie Holiday

Bossy Kelis

Bravo Ledisi

Cactus Tree Joni Mitchell

Call Me (Come Back Home) Al Green

Can't Hold Us Down Christina Aguilera featuring Lil' Kim

Can't Stop Fighting Sheer Mag

Can You Deal? Bleached

Chains and Things B. B. King

Cheek to Cheek Ella Fitzgerald

Cinderella Play

Confident Demi Lovato

Could've Been H.E.R. (featuring Bryson Tiller)

Dance Apocalyptic Janelle Monáe

Dancing in The Street Martha Reeves and the Vandellas

Darn That Dream Ella Fitzgerald

Disco Yes Tom Misch (featuring Poppy Ajudha)

Don't Stop 'Til You Get Enough Michael Jackson

Don't You Know That? Luther Vandross

Doo Wop (That Thing) Ms. Lauryn Hill

Dream a Little Dream of Me Ella Fitzgerald

Dreams Gary Wilson

Easy Livin' Billie Holiday

Ekombe Jupiter and Okwess

Endless Love Lionel Richie, Diana Ross

End of the Road Boyz II Men

E Pluribus Unum The Last Poets

Every Time I Hear That Song Brandi Carlile

Express Yourself Charles Wright and the Watts 103rd Street Rhythm Band

Fallin' Alicia Keys

Family Beyoncé, Jamie Foxx, Keith Robinson, Anika Noni Rose, Jennifer Hudson (from the soundtrack to *Dreamgirls*)

Fancy Lady Billy Preston

Feeding Off the Love of the Land Stevie Wonder

Feeling Good Nina Simone

Feeling Myself Nicki Minaj, Beyoncé

Fightin' Fire with Fire The Bar-Kays

Formation Beyoncé

For Once in My Life Stevie Wonder

Freedom Beyoncé

Get Ur Freak On Missy Elliott

Girl, I Think the World about You Commodores

Girl on Fire Alicia Keys

God Is a Woman Ariana Grande

Gone Baby, Don't Be Long Erykah Badu

Good Times Chic

Grown Woman Beyoncé

Halo Beyoncé

Happy Pharell

Harder Better Faster Stronger Daft Punk

Hard Out Here Lily Allen

Heard It All Before Sunshine Anderson

Heaven John Legend

Heaven Bound Rufus featuring Chaka Khan

Hello It's Me The Isley Brothers

Hold On En Vogue

Hold Up Beyoncé

Hollaback Girl Gwen Stefani

How High the Moon (1st Take) Ella Fitzgerald

Hot Topic Le Tigre

Human Nature Madonna

Humble Kendrick Lamar

I Am Woman Betty Wright

I Did It All Tracy Chapman

I Found You Alabama Shakes

I Heard It through the Grapevine Gladys Knight and The Pips

I'm Every Woman Chaka Khan

In the Midnight Hour Gary Wilson

Independent Women, Pt. 1 Destiny's Child

I Never Loved a Man (The Way I Love You) Aretha Franklin

Into Each Life Some Rain Must Fall Ella Fitzgerald

I Put a Spell on You Nina Simone

Isn't She Lovely Stevie Wonder

It Takes Two Marvin Gaye, Kim Weston

I Wanna Dance with Somebody (Who Loves Me) Whitney Houston

I Want You Back Jackson Five

I Was Here Beyoncé

I Will Survive Gloria Gaynor

Just a Girl No Doubt

Just Fine Mary J. Blige

Kool Thing Sonic Youth

Let's Dance David Bowie

Let's Stay Together Al Green

Like You'll Never See Me Again Janelle Monáe

Little Red Corvette (Dance Mix) Prince

Living for the City Stevie Wonder

Love Drought Beyoncé

Love Is Here to Stay Ella Fitzgerald and Louis Armstrong

Love Myself Hailee Steinfeld

Make Me Feel Janelle Monáe

Man! I Feel Like a Woman Shania Twain

Mary Don't You Weep (Piano and a Microphone 1983 Version) Prince

Men Explain Things to Me Tacocat

Miss Independent Kelly Clarkson

Monstro Downtown Boys

More Than Anything in This World Lenny Kravitz

My Baby Just Cares for Me Nina Simone

My Love Is Your Love Whitney Houston

My Own Thing Chance the Rapper (featuring Joey Purp)

My Guy Mary Wells

My Shot Lin-Manuel Miranda, Anthony Ramos, Daveed Diggs, Okieriete Onaodowan, Leslie Odom Jr., Original Broadway Cast of *Hamilton*

Natural Woman Aretha Franklin

Need a Little Time Courtney Barnett

New Rules Dua Lipa

Never Too Much Luther Vandross

Nina Cried Power Hozier (featuring Mavis Staples)

No Diggity Blackstreet

None of Your Business
Salt-N-Pepa

No Scrubs TLC

On the Sunny Side of the Street Billie Holiday

Ordinary People John Legend

Please Mr. Postman
The Marvelettes

Pink + White Frank Ocean

Py Grabs Back**
Kim Boekbinder

Q.U.E.E.N. Janelle Monáe and Erykah Badu

Quiet MILCK

Rebel Girl Bikini Kill

Reflection Lea Salonga

Remember the Time
Michael Jackson

Respect Aretha Franklin

Rhythm Nation Janet Jackson

Riot Miles Davis

Rock with You
Michael Jackson

Rock Steady Aretha Franklin

Rolling in the Deep Adele

Runnin' Earth, Wind and Fire

Run the World (Girls)
Beyoncé

Señorita Justin Timberlake

Signed, Sealed, Delivered (I'm Yours) Stevie Wonder

Sign O' the Times Prince

Single Ladies (Put A Ring On It) Beyoncé

Sinnerman Nina Simone

Sir Duke Stevie Wonder

Sisters Are Doin' It For Themselves Eurythmics and Aretha Franklin

So Amazing Luther Vandross

Someday We'll Be Together
Diana Ross and The Supremes

Something in the Way She Moves James Taylor

So You're Leaving Al Green

Sorry Beyoncé

Strange Fruit Billie Holiday

Summertime DJ Jazzy Jeff and The Fresh Prince

Superwoman Karyn White

Survivor Destiny's Child

Sweet Home Chicago
Robert Johnson

Take Off the Blues
The Foreign Exchange, Darien Brockington

Talkin 'Bout a Revolution
Tracy Chapman

Tell Me I'm Not Dreaming (Too Good to Be True)
Jermaine Jackson, Michael Jackson

The Best Tina Turner

The Boy Is Mine Brandy, Monica

The Door D'Angelo

The Future Is Female
Madame Gandhi
(TT the Artist Club Remix featuring UNIIQU3)

The Gospel Alicia Keys

The Man I Love Ella Fitzgerald

The Old Heart of Mine (Is Weak for You) The Isley Brothers

The Pill Loretta Lynn

The Very Thought of You
Billie Holiday

The Way You Do the Things You Do The Temptations

Thinking of You Sister Sledge

This Is America
Childish Gambino

This Is For My Girls
Missy Elliott, Kelly Clarkson, Zendaya, Kelly Rowland, Janelle Monáe, Lea Michele, Jadagrace, and Chloe & Halle

This Is Serious Lunachicks

This One's for the Girls
Martina McBride

This Will Be (An Everlasting Love) Natalie Cole

Thriller Michael Jackson

Tightrope Janelle Monáe

To Be Young, Gifted and Black Nina Simone

Treat Her Like A Lady
The Temptations

Tummy Ache Diet Cig

Typical Girls The Slits

U.N.I.T.Y. Queen Latifah

Unbreakable Alicia Keys

Uptown Funk Mark Ronson featuring Bruno Mars

Video India Arie

What a Wonderful World
Louis Armstrong

What a World Common

What Goes Around Comes Around Lenny Kravitz

Wonder Woman Lion Babe

Woman Kesha featuring The Dap-Kings Horns

Workin' Overtime Diana Ross

You and I (Nobody in the World) John Legend

You Don't Know My Name
Alicia Keys

You Don't Own Me Leslie Gore

You Get Me Peven Everett

You're Gonna Need Me
Dionne Warwick

You Gotta Believe Rose Royce, The Pointer Sisters

You're My Thrill Billie Holiday

You Send Me Sam Cooke

You Will Rise Sweetback

You've Got the Love I Need
Al Green, Anthony Hamilton

COLOR-IN US ELECTION MAP 2008

On November 4, 2008, Barack Obama defeated Republican candidate John McCain in the 56th quadrennial presidential election and became the first African-American President.

Color in the map following the number key below to show how the individual states voted.

2008 RESULT

1 Landslide Democrat win
COLOR IN DARK BLUE

2 Firm Democrat win
COLOR IN MEDIUM BLUE

3 Moderate Democrat win
COLOR IN LIGHT BLUE

4 Narrow Democrat win
COLOR IN VERY PALE BLUE

5 Landslide Republican win
COLOR IN DARK RED

6 Firm Republican win
COLOR IN MEDIUM RED

7 Moderate Republican win
COLOR IN LIGHT RED

8 Narrow Republican win
COLOR IN VERY PALE RED

2008 RESULTS

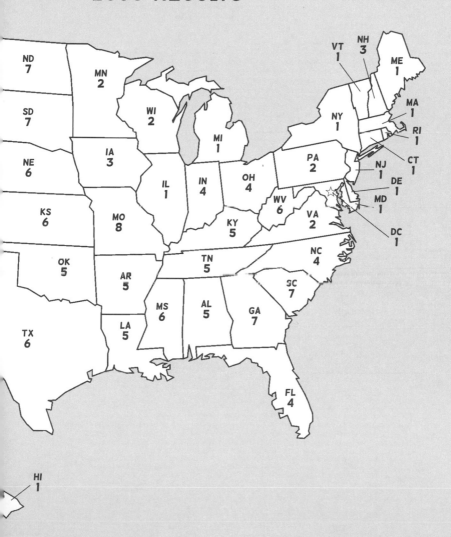

ND 7

MN 2

SD 7

WI 2

MI 1

VT 1

NH 3

ME 1

NY 1

MA 1

RI 1

CT 1

NE 6

IA 3

PA 2

NJ 1

DE 1

KS 6

MO 8

IL 1

IN 4

OH 4

WV 6

VA 2

MD 1

DC 1

OK 5

AR 5

KY 5

TN 5

NC 4

SC 7

TX 6

LA 5

MS 6

AL 5

GA 7

FL 4

HI 1

THE OBAMAS: A Love Story

Michelle and Barack's first official date as a couple involved a trip to Chicago's Art Institute, followed by a cinema outing to see Spike Lee's new film *Do the Right Thing*.

Then potential disaster struck.

Michelle and Barack bumped into one of the company's senior partners, Newt Minow, and his wife Josephine in the popcorn queue. Nightmare. But, slightly to Michelle's surprise (clearly not buying point e in Barack's arguments in favor of them dating, on page 56), Newt and Josephine greeted Michelle and Barack warmly.

Michelle's assistant Lorraine had also figured out what was going on, giving Barack knowing smiles every time he appeared at Michelle's door.

Michelle began staying over at Barack's home—a second-floor apartment above a storefront that he was subletting from a University of Chicago law student. The apartment was on a noisy section of 53rd Street in Chicago's Hyde Park neighborhood, close to the university.

Michelle recalls waking up one night to find Barack illuminated by the glow of the streetlights behind. He looked like he was thinking about something deeply personal. Michelle mused that it might be their relationship or losing his father. She asked him, receiving the reply:

"Oh, I was just thinking about income inequality."

Michelle has described Barack as a unicorn on more than
one occasion, so we thought we'd oblige her imagination.
Also, this is how you should have to enter the White House
when you're sworn in as president.

SIX DEGREES OF
KEVIN BACON

Can you link Michelle Obama to Dick Van Dyke in four moves or less?
Remember that animated films count!

And when you're done with that, try linking Michelle Obama with Julie
Andrews in five moves or less. We're giving you the first link (Michelle
appeared on *The Tonight Show with Jimmy Fallon* several times).

PERSON	FILM / TV SHOW
1 Ellen DeGeneres	*The Ellen DeGeneres Show*
2	
3 Dick Van Dyke	

PERSON	FILM / TV SHOW
1 Jimmy Fallon	*The Tonight Show*
2	
3	
4	
5 Julie Andrews	

US POLITICS CROSSWORD

DOWN

1 What is the name for the practice of redrawing the boundaries of electoral districts to give a party an advantage?

2 What is the third largest political party in the US?

3 Who was the president of the United States during the American Civil War?

4 What is the name of the presidential retreat in Maryland?

5 1600 Pennsylvania Avenue is the address of which building?

7 What is the name of the Republican Party movement founded in 2009, whose name references a famous anti-British protest in 1773?

9 Which month are general elections held in the United States?

ACROSS

6 Which US president appears on the front of a $1 bill?

8 How many justices of the Supreme Court are there?

10 In 2012, two states became the first to legalize marijuana for recreational use. Washington was one of them. What was the other?

11 What did the 13th amendment to the US Constitution, passed in Congress in 1865, abolish?

12 Complete the following quote from the Declaration of Independence: "Life, -------, and the Pursuit of Happiness."

FAMOUS HUG RECIPIENTS

Michelle's hugs are legendary.
Here are some surprising recipients.

The Queen
(A breach of protocol)

This was called a "breach of royal protocol" by some UK newspapers, but the Queen showed a similar disregard for convention by putting her arm around Michelle's back. According to Michelle, the pair bonded over their hurting feet before sharing a hearty laugh. So perhaps the calls to lock Michelle up in the Tower of London were overdoing it slightly…

George W. Bush
(An unlikely affection)

Michelle and George have shared many sweet moments over the years. "President Bush and I, we are forever seatmates because of protocol, and that's how we sit at all the official functions. He's my partner in crime at every major thing where all the 'formers' gather. So we're together all the time." She later said, "I love him to death. He's a wonderful man, he's a funny man."

Prince Harry
(Fan boy!)

Michelle famously surprised guests at a 2013 White House Mother's Day tea for members of the US military by introducing Harry to the crowd, much to their delight. You can tell he's quite a fan of the former First Lady.

Silvio Berlusconi handshake
(Keep your distance!)

At the 2009 G20 Summit in Pittsburgh, Michelle kept Italian Prime Minister Silvio Berlusconi (embroiled in multiple scandals involving call girls and in the process of being divorced by his wife) at arm's length. Good call!

Melania Trump
(Warmth trumps formality)

At Donald Trump's inauguration in 2009, Melania extended her hand, but Michelle offered a warmer gesture, leaning in for a kiss and a hug. Elegance, grace and charm (in painful circumstances).

BECOMING 2019 TOUR: DATES, VENUES, AND MODERATORS

DATE	LOCATION	VENUE	CAPACITY	MODERATOR
February 8	Tacoma, Washington	Tacoma Dome	23,000	Jimmy Kimmel
February 9	Portland, Oregon	Moda Center	19,980	Phoebe Robinson
February 12	Phoenix, Arizona	Comerica Theatre	5,000	Valerie Jarrett
February 28	Austin, Texas	Frank Erwin Center	16,734	Rachel Ray
March 2	Houston, Texas	Toyota Center	18,300	Michele Norris
March 13	St Paul, Minnesota	Xcel Energy Center	20,554	Michele Norris
March 14	Milwaukee, Wisconsin	Miller High Life Theatre	4,086	Conan O'Brien
March 16	Cleveland, Ohio	KeyBank State Theatre	3,400	Carla Hall

DATE	LOCATION	VENUE	CAPACITY	MODERATOR
March 19	Portland, Oregon	Moda Center	19,980	Sam Kass
March 21	Vancouver, British Columbia, Canada	Rogers Arena	18,910	Robin Roberts
March 22	Edmonton, Alberta, Canada	Rogers Place	20,734	Robin Roberts
March 24	Tacoma, Washington	Tacoma Dome	23,000	Jimmy Kimmel
Apr 9	Copenhagen, Denmark	Royal Arena	16,000	Rachel Ray
Apr 10	Stockholm, Sweden	Ericsson Globe	16,000	Phoebe Robinson
Apr 11	Oslo, Norway	Oslo Spektrum	9,700	Phoebe Robinson
Apr 14	London, UK	The O2 Arena	20,000	Stephen Colbert
Apr 16	Paris, France	AccorHotels Arena	20,300	Isha Sesay
Apr 17	Amsterdam, Netherlands	Ziggo Dome	17,000	Isha Sesay
May 3	Montreal, Quebec, Canada	Bell Centre	21,273	Valerie Jarrett
May 4	Toronto, Ontario, Canada	Scotiabank Arena	19,800	Phoebe Robinson
May 10	Ft. Lauderdale, Florida	BB&T Center	20,737	Jessica Williams
May 11	Atlanta, Georgia	State Farm Arena	21,000	Gayle King
May 12	Nashville, Tennessee	Ryman Auditorium	2,362	Stephen Colbert

Design Your Own
Michelle Obama
BANKNOTE

You've been asked to liven up the $10 bill, the front of which currently features Alexander Hamilton. What did Hamilton ever do anyway, except star in a hit Broadway show? So, please set to work designing a new banknote that Michelle would be proud of.

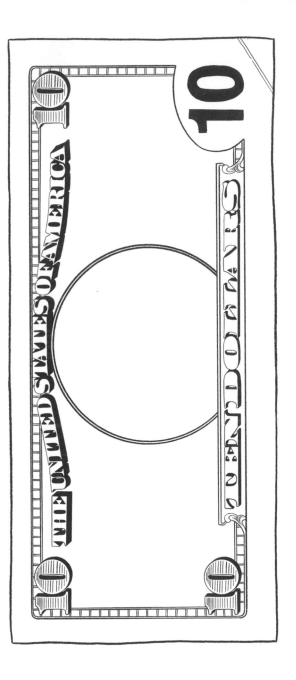

Dot-to-dot Michelle

Join the dots to locate Michelle with James Corden and Missy Elliott for a special edition of *Carpool Karaoke*.

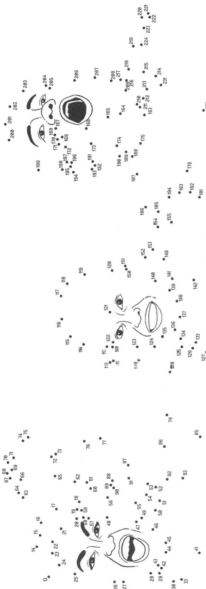

SPOT THE DIFFERENCE

Can you spot the seven differences
between this picture of
Air Force One and the
one opposite?

In 2009, author and genealogist Megan Smolenyak traced back Michelle's bloodline to a slave from South Carolina named Melvinia. She was Michelle's great-great-great-grandmother. Then, in 2012, the *New York Times* journalist Rachel Swarns discovered that Melvinia became pregnant, aged 15, by 20-year-old Charles Shields, the son of one of her owners. She had a mixed-race son named Dolphus T. Shields, the former First Lady's great-great-grandfather.

Charles Shields' father, Henry Wells Shields, was a cotton farmer descended from Andrew Shields, a Protestant Irish immigrant who fought in the American Revolutionary War (1775–83) against the British.

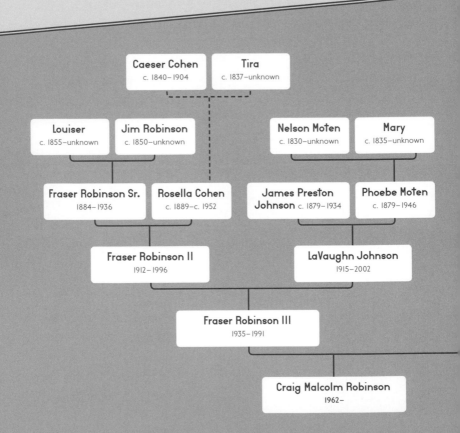

Caeser Cohen
c. 1840–1904

Tira
c. 1837–unknown

Louiser
c. 1855–unknown

Jim Robinson
c. 1850–unknown

Nelson Moten
c. 1830–unknown

Mary
c. 1835–unknown

Fraser Robinson Sr.
1884–1936

Rosella Cohen
c. 1889–c. 1952

James Preston Johnson c. 1879–1934

Phoebe Moten
c. 1879–1946

Fraser Robinson II
1912–1996

LaVaughn Johnson
1915–2002

Fraser Robinson III
1935–1991

Craig Malcolm Robinson
1962–

In 2009, Megan Smolenyak also traced Barack's heritage. His maternal great-great-great-grandfather was Falmouth Kearney from Moneygall in central Ireland. In 1850, Kearney, then a nineteen-year-old son of a shoemaker, left Ireland to start a new life in the United States. In 2011, Barack and Michelle visited the village and memorably enjoyed pints of Guinness. At a reception in Dublin later that day, Barack said, "My name is Barack Obama, of the Moneygall O'Bamas. I've come home to find the apostrophe that we lost somewhere along the way."

Here is Michelle's family tree as far as it can be traced back.

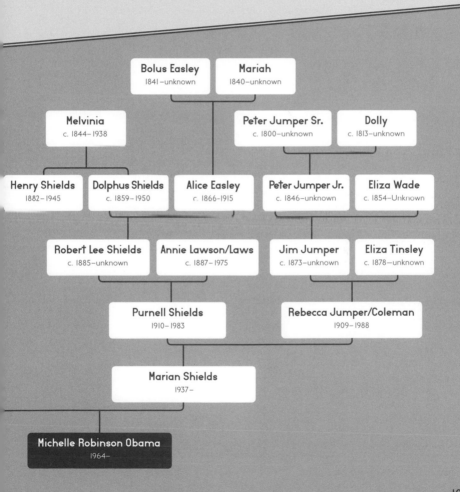

Final State Dinner

The fourteenth and final state dinner of the Obama administration was held on the South Lawn in October 2016. The Obamas hosted Italian Prime Minister Matteo Renzi and his wife Agnese. Here's what was on the menu.

MENU

PASSED CANAPÉS

Hamachi Agrodolce with recently harvested eggplant from the White House Kitchen Garden

Roasted figs with speck and herb pesto made from the garden's cinnamon basil

Crab cannolis with homegrown currant tomatoes

Grilled rosemary lamb with freshly picked rosemary

FIRST COURSE

Sweet potato Agnolotti "a velvety pillow of paper-thin pasta" stuffed with sweet potatoes, garnished with nutmeg and parsley, and topped with browned butter and sage

SECOND COURSE

Warm butternut squash salad topped with bitter chicory, preserved pumpkin, shaved ewe's milk cheese from New York, and raw apple cider vinaigrette made with olive oil from California

MAIN COURSE

Beef Braciole Pinwheel, with prime tenderloin layered with bresaola, fontina cheese, parsley, garlic, and panko breadcrumbs, served atop broccoli rabe, garnished with horseradish gremolata, apple matchsticks, and arugula

DESSERT

Green apple crostata, with a flaky and delicate crust filled with semolina batter and lightly poached green apple, topped with thyme caramel sauce, crunchy toffee crumble, and buttermilk gelato

"Celebrating Autumn's Harvest" platter with mini pastries including a sweet corn crema and blackberry cup, a Concord grape chocolate leaf, orange and fig slices, a pumpkin cranberry tart, and tiramisu

THE OBAMA FOUNDATION

The Obama Foundation was founded in 2014 and guided by the core belief that "ordinary people working together can change history". The Foundation's mission is to inspire, empower, and connect people so they can take action and make the world a better place.

The Foundation runs **My Brother's Keeper Alliance**, a project founded in February 2014 to help young people reach their dreams regardless of race, color, gender, or socioeconomic status. It also runs **Global Girls Alliance**, a program unveiled by Michelle in October 2018 that seeks to empower adolescent girls across the world through education so they can reach their potential.

The Foundation also operates the **Obama Foundation Fellowship** to support twenty community-minded people for a two-year program to help amplify their work through collaboration with like-minded people and potential partners.

The Foundation works in partnership with the **University of Chicago**, awarding twenty-five scholarships to students at the Harris School of Public Policy to study for a masters in international development and policy.

The Foundation will oversee the creation of the **Barack Obama Presidential Center**, which will be built near the University of Chicago and will house a presidential library to preserve the papers, records, and collections of the Obama administration.

Find the Speech Maze

Donald Trump has spitefully stolen Michelle's speech for an upcoming fundraiser and hidden it in a maze that he's shaped in his own likeness. He's left it at the end of the maze along with his hairpiece, which must have blown off in the wind. Can you find the speech?

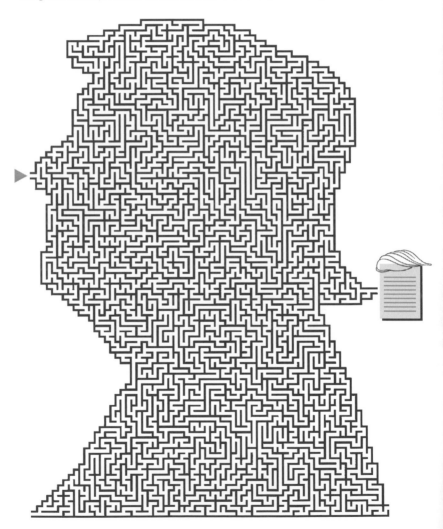

WHERE'S MICHELLE?

Can you spot our heroine (in miniature) among the contents of this famous British royal palace?

"Even though back then Barack was a senator and a presidential candidate... to me, he was still the guy who'd picked me up for our dates in a car that was so rusted out, I could actually see the pavement going by through a hole in the passenger–side door... he was the guy whose proudest possession was a coffee table he'd found in a dumpster, and whose only pair of decent shoes was half a size too small."

Michelle deftly painting a picture of her husband's values and resourcefulness in her speech to the Democratic National Convention, 2012

Friendship

"Do not bring people in your life who weigh you down. And trust your instincts ... good relationships feel good. They feel right. They don't hurt. They're not painful. That's not just with somebody you want to marry, but it's with the friends that you choose. It's with the people you surround yourselves with."

VISIT TO ELIZABETH GARRETT ANDERSON SCHOOL, LONDON, UK, 2011

"Walk away from 'friendships' that make you feel small and insecure, and seek out people who inspire you and support you."

PEOPLE MAGAZINE, 2014

"I see a lot of men laughing, but y'all need to go talk to each other about your stuff, because there's so much of it, it's so messy! Just talk about why you all are the way you are."

ON HOW BARACK COULD USE A FEW MORE FRIENDS, OBAMA FOUNDATION SUMMIT, 2017

"We should always have three friends in our lives—one who walks ahead who we look up to and follow; one who walks beside us, who is with us every step of our journey; and then, one who we reach back for and bring along after we've cleared the way."

NATIONAL MENTORING SUMMIT, 2011

"We're all Americans. We all care about our family and our kids, and we're trying to get ahead. And that's how I feel about your father. You know?"

TALKING TO JENNA BUSH HAGER ABOUT HER FRIENDSHIP WITH GEORGE W. BUSH, 2018

"I love my husband, and he is my rock, but my girlfriends are my sanity."

OBAMA FOUNDATION SUMMIT, 2017

Highs and Lows

- Michelle joined law firm Sidley Austin in June 1988 as an associate specializing in intellectual property. The following summer, Michelle was asked to mentor a young summer associate by the name of Barack Hussein Obama.

- Michelle's dear friend from college, Suzanne Alele, developed an aggressive form of lymphoma and died at age 26 in June 1990.

- Michelle's father, Fraser Robinson III, having suffered from multiple sclerosis for many years, was admitted to hospital in February 1991. Tragically, he died ten days later, at age 55, of a heart attack.

- Shortly after her father's death, Michelle decided that she didn't want to spend her life writing legal briefs and defending corporate trademarks. She was introduced to Valerie Jarrett, the deputy chief of staff to the mayor of Chicago, who offered Michelle a job.

- Barack graduated from Harvard Law School in late May 1991, packed up his things, sold his rusted yellow Datsun, and moved back to Chicago.

- Barack was approached by a literary agent, who secured a $40,000 book deal for Barack to write what became his bestselling book about race and identity, *Dreams from My Father* (1995).

- Michelle took and failed the Illinois Bar Exam, the first time she had ever failed a test (except for a time in kindergarten where she failed to read the word *white* off a card held up by the teacher). She passed the exam the second time around.

- Barack took the Illinois Bar Exam on July 31, 1991, and he and Michelle celebrated at a restaurant in downtown Chicago. Barack decided that it was the right time to bring up the subject of marriage, declaring that as much as he loved her, he didn't see the point. Michelle provided a spirited defense for the institution of marriage, going into clauses and sub-clauses, which lasted some time, until dessert arrived.

- Rather than the chocolate cake that Michelle had ordered, she was presented with a platter containing a velvet box. Barack opened the box to reveal a diamond engagement ring and said "Now that ought to shut you up." That wily unicorn had been pulling her leg all along!

- Michelle accepted both Barack's proposal and Valerie's job offer to work at city hall as an assistant to Mayor Richard M. Daley.

- In August 1991, Barack and Michelle traveled to Nairobi, Kenya, to meet Barack's half-sister Auma and his grandmother Sarah.

Trumps vs. Obamas

At Trump's inauguration on January 20, 2017, an image was snapped that highlighted the fairly stark difference between the two couples.

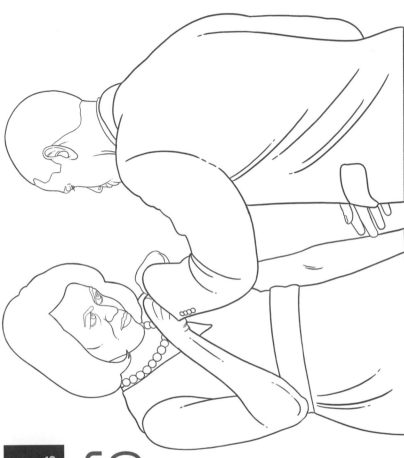

COLOR-IN
RELATIONSHIP GOALS

Yes We can (fist-bump)

After finding out that he had secured the Democratic nomination for president in Minnesota in June 2008, Barack and Michelle shared this pricelessly affectionate moment.

WORD CLOUD

MICHELLE'S SPEECH TO THE DEMOCRATIC NATIONAL CONVENTION IN 2012

On September 4, 2012, Michelle delivered a passionate, persuasive, and heartfelt keynote address to open the Democratic National Convention, making the case for her husband's reelection. CNN described it as "one of the finest speeches ever delivered at a national political convention."

COLOR-IN US ELECTION MAP 2012

On November 6, 2012, Barack Obama defeated Republican candidate Mitt Romney in the fifty-seventh quadrennial presidential election.

Color in the map following the number key below to show how the individual states voted.

2012 RESULT

1 Landslide Democrat win
COLOR IN DARK BLUE

2 Firm Democrat win
COLOR IN MEDIUM BLUE

3 Moderate Democrat win
COLOR IN LIGHT BLUE

4 Narrow Democrat win
COLOR IN VERY PALE BLUE

5 Landslide Republican win
COLOR IN DARK RED

6 Firm Republican win
COLOR IN MEDIUM RED

7 Moderate Republican win
COLOR IN LIGHT RED

8 Narrow Republican win
COLOR IN VERY PALE RED

2012 RESULTS

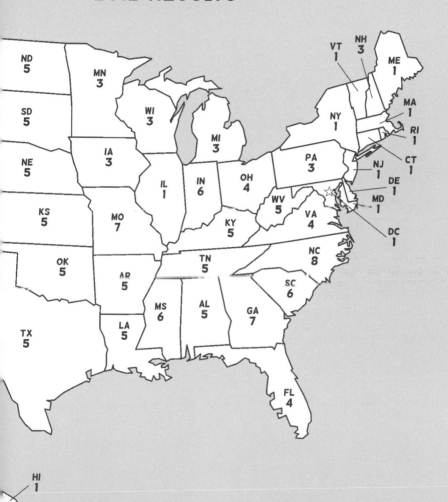

ND
5

MN
3

SD
5

WI
3

MI
3

NE
5

IA
3

IL
1

IN
6

OH
4

PA
3

NY
1

VT
1

NH
3

ME
1

MA
1

RI
1

CT
1

NJ
1

DE
1

MD
1

DC
1

WV
5

VA
4

KS
5

MO
7

KY
5

OK
5

AR
5

TN
5

NC
8

SC
6

TX
5

LA
5

MS
6

AL
5

GA
7

FL
4

HI
1

Tallest First Ladies

Here are the ten tallest First Ladies assembled in a *Usual Suspects*–style gallery that makes them look like criminals. Now, Michelle and Melania are both officially 5 foot, 11 inches (1.8 meters), but in the photos at Donald Trump's inauguration, Michelle definitely has the edge (in so many ways).

Eleanor Roosevelt
5 foot, 11 inches
(1.8 meters)

Melania Trump
5 foot, 11 inches
(1.8 meters)

Michelle Obama
5 foot, 11 inches
(1.8 meters)

Edith Wilson
5 foot, 9 inches
(1.75 meters)

Jackie Kennedy
5 foot, 8 inches
(1.73 meters)

Lou Hoover
5 foot, 8 inches
(1.73 meters)

Dolley Madison
5 foot, 7 inches
(1.7 meters)

Edith Roosevelt
5 foot, 7 inches
(1.7 meters)

Florence Harding
5 foot, 7 inches
(1.7 meters)

Tallest Presidents

Here are the nine tallest Presidents.
The average height for a US President is 5 foot, 10 inches
(1.78 meters).

Abraham Lincoln
6 foot, 4 inches
(1.93 meters)

Lyndon B. Johnson
6 foot, 3½ inches
(1.92 meters)

Donald Trump
6 foot, 3 inches
(1.91 meters)

Thomas Jefferson
6 foot, 2½ inches
(1.89 meters)

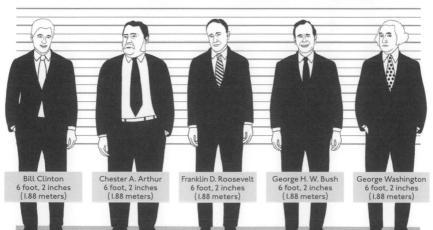

Bill Clinton
6 foot, 2 inches
(1.88 meters)

Chester A. Arthur
6 foot, 2 inches
(1.88 meters)

Franklin D. Roosevelt
6 foot, 2 inches
(1.88 meters)

George H. W. Bush
6 foot, 2 inches
(1.88 meters)

George Washington
6 foot, 2 inches
(1.88 meters)

MATCH THE CHILD'S NAME TO THE FIRST FAMILY

Only one child has been born in the White House: Esther Cleveland, the daughter of Frances and Grover Cleveland (in office 1885–89 and 1893–97). Two presidents married while in office: John Tyler (in office 1841–45) and Woodrow Wilson (in office 1913–21), who remarried in 1915.

Can you link the child's name to the name of the first family?

CHILD	FIRST FAMILY
BARRON	The Nixons
CHELSEA	The H. W. Bushes
JEB	The Clintons
PATTI	The Trumps
TRICIA	The Kennedys
CAROLINE	The Carters
JENNA	The Obamas
SASHA	The W. Bushes
LYNDA BIRD	The Reagans
AMY	The Johnsons

MATCH THE FAITHFUL FRIEND TO THE FIRST FAMILY

Andrew Jackson owned a gray parrot, but it learned how to swear and had to be ejected from Jackson's funeral owing to repeated profanity. You can't make this stuff up! Find out if you can match the faithful friends to the first family (that's a tongue twister if ever I heard one). We've given you some clues, because otherwise some of these are quite tricky.

PET	FIRST FAMILY	CLUE
SUNNY (Portuguese water dog)	The Nixons	Introduced to the world via Twitter
BUDDY (Labrador retriever)	The H. W. Bushes	Did not get along with the couple's other pet, Socks the cat
CHECKERS (cocker spaniel)	The Clintons	Mentioned in a famous political speech in 1952
FIDO (mutt)	The D. Roosevelts	Assassinated, like its owner
FAITHFUL (Newfoundland)	The Johnsons	Civil War commanding general
FALA (Scottish terrier)	The Lincolns	Famously left behind when the President visited the Aleutian Islands in 1944
BARNEY (Scottish terrier)	The Fords	Had his own official webpage
MILLIE (springer spaniel)	The W. Bushes	Her owner once uttered, "My dog Millie knows more about foreign affairs than these two bozos," in reference to Al Gore and Bill Clinton
LIBERTY (golden retriever)	The S. Grants	Shortest-serving president who didn't die in office
HIM AND HER (beagles)	The Obamas	President often referred to by his initials

First Lady of Fitness

"[Being fit] has become even more important as I've had children, because I'm also thinking about how I'm modeling health to my daughters. I'm trying to teach my daughters moderation and constancy, that exercise is not a luxury, it is a necessity."

EBONY, 2008

"Parents have a right to expect that their efforts at home won't be undone each day in the school cafeteria or the vending machine in the hallway ... Parents have a right to expect that their kids will be served fresh, healthy food that meets high nutritional standards."

SIGNING OF THE HEALTHY, HUNGER-FREE KIDS ACT, 2010

"The physical and emotional health of an entire generation and the economic health and security of our nation is at stake. This isn't the kind of problem that can be solved overnight, but with everyone working together, it can be solved. So, let's move."

LET'S MOVE! LAUNCH ANNOUNCEMENT, 2010

"With every healthy meal and snack you provide for kids in your community, you're not just nourishing them today; you are shaping their habits and their tastes for the rest of their lives."

LET'S MOVE! CITIES, TOWNS AND COUNTIES, 2015

"[Exercise] makes me feel good. It gives me energy, you know? ... There's something about exercise that gets your heart pumping and the blood running that actually makes me feel better. And when I don't exercise a lot, I start feeling sluggish and more tired. And I don't know about you, but I want to live a long time, okay? I want to be ... a 90-year-old lady that's really fly."

Q&A AT TAKE OUR DAUGHTERS AND SONS TO WORK DAY, APRIL 2016

First Lady of Fitness
MICHELLE'S
WORKOUT PLAYLIST

In May 2012, Michelle revealed the songs that keep her in shape to *Women's Health* magazine. It took Barack another four years to reveal his, when he guest-edited *Wired* magazine. See what you think!

MICHELLE

 "Signed, Sealed, Delivered (I'm Yours)" — Stevie Wonder

2   "Move Your Body" — Beyoncé

3   "Tightrope" (feat. Big Boi) — Janelle Monáe

4   "Love Song" — Sara Bareilles

5   "Unbreakable" — Michael Jackson

6   "Whip My Hair" — Willow

7   "I Was Here" — Beyoncé

8   "Treat 'Em Right" — Chubb Rock

9   "Thank You" — Ledisi

10   "Get Right" — Jennifer Lopez

BARACK

 "Let's Get It Started" — The Black Eyed Peas

2   "Sinnerman" — Nina Simone

3   "If You Love Somebody Set Them Free" — Sting

4   "Live It Up, Pts 1 & 2" — The Isley Brothers

5   "Emergency" — Icona Pop

6   "Perro Loco" — Forro In The Dark

7   "Get Me Bodied" — Beyoncé

8   "Off That" — Jay-Z

9   "Could You Be Loved" — Bob Marley & The Wailers

10   "Elevator Operator" — Courtney Barnett

FAMOUS FIRSTS FOR AFRICAN AMERICANS

First to earn a bachelor's degree
ALEXANDER LUCIUS TWILIGHT (1795–1857), who graduated from Middlebury College, Vermont, in 1823

First woman to earn a Bachelor's degree
MARY JANE PATTERSON (1840–1894), who graduated from Oberlin College, Ohio, in 1862

First state-elected official
ALEXANDER LUCIUS TWILIGHT (1795–1857), who was elected to the Vermont House of Representatives in 1836

First female state-elected official
MINNIE BUCKINGHAM HARPER (1886–1978), who was elected to the West Virginia House of Delegates in 1929

First mayor of a major city
CARL STOKES (1927–1996), who became the Mayor of Cleveland, Ohio, in November 1967 and served until 1971

First female mayor of a major city
LOTTIE SHACKELFORD (1941–), who was elected mayor of Little Rock, Arkansas, in 1987 and served until 1988

First elected governor
L. DOUGLAS WILDER (1931–), who became governor of Virginia in November 1990 and served until 1994

First member of the US House of Representatives
JOSEPH RAINEY (1832–1887), who became a congressman from South Carolina in December 1870 and served until 1879

First female member of the US House of Representatives
SHIRLEY CHISHOLM (1924–2005), who became a congresswoman from New York in January 1969 and served until 1983

First member of the US Senate

HIRAM REVELS (1827–1901), who became a senator for Mississippi in February 1870 and served until March 1871

First female member of the US Senate

CAROL MOSELEY BRAUN (1947–), who became a senator for Illinois in January 1993 and served until 1999

First member of the US Cabinet

ROBERT C. WEAVER (1907–1997), who was appointed secretary of the department of Housing and Urban Development by Lyndon B. Johnson in January 1966

First female member of the US Cabinet

PATRICIA ROBERTS HARRIS (1927–1985), who in January 1977 was appointed secretary of the Department of Housing and Urban Development by Jimmy Carter

First secretary of state

COLIN POWELL (1937–), who was appointed by George W. Bush in 2001 and served until 2005

First female secretary of state

CONDOLEEZZA RICE (1954–), who was appointed by George W. Bush in 2005 and served until 2009

First party nominee for president

BARACK OBAMA (1961–), who was nominated by the Democratic Party in June 2008

First federal judge

WILLIAM HENRY HASTIE (1904–1976), who was appointed a federal judge by Harry S. Truman in October 1949

First female federal judge

CONSTANCE BAKER MOTLEY (1921–2005), who was nominated a federal judge by Lyndon B. Johnson in January 1966

First justice of the supreme court

THURGOOD MARSHALL (1908–1993), who was appointed an associate justice of the Supreme Court in October 1967 and served until 1991

First president

BARACK OBAMA (1961–), who was elected following the election on November 4, 2008

First first lady

MICHELLE OBAMA (1964–), who became First Lady following the election of Barack on November 4, 2008

FIRST LADY
ANAGRAMS

Can you unscramble the ludicrous words below
to reveal the names of former first ladies?

ARUBA LUSH _____

PLATINUM MARE_____

CHILLY TORN NAIL _____

HOOVERED TILES _____

PAN TOXIN _____

ABLE CHAMOMILE _____

BAA RHUBARBS _____

ANNY CARNAGE _____

CINDY JAKE KEEN _____

DERBY TOFT _____

ELEVATOR LOOSENER _____

MARATHONS THAWING _____

Dot-to-dot Michelle

Join the dots to reveal Michelle's priceless expression at Donald Trump's inauguration.

Newlyweds

Barack and Michelle were married at Trinity United Church of Christ on October 3, 1992, in South Side Chicago in front of over 300 friends and family. Santita Jackson was her maid of honor. Barack had woken up with a terrible cold, but it seemed to clear as he arrived at the church dressed in a rented tuxedo and a shiny pair of new shoes.

Their reception was held at the South Shore Cultural Center. Their wedding song was Stevie Wonder's "You and I (We Can Conquer the World)," a track from the first album Michelle had been given by her late grandfather, Southside Shields. Their first dance was to Nat King Cole's "Unforgettable."

The Obamas spent their honeymoon in Northern California in the Napa Valley before road-tripping along the Big Sur coast. We don't need the full details, but we do know that they spent a lot of time reading and staring at the Pacific Ocean. And possibly drank the odd glass of wine.

- Barack had spent most of the year 1992 spearheading Project VOTE! in Illinois, tasked with signing up an estimated 400,000 unregistered African-American voters.

- Michelle was offered the job of assistant commissioner in charge of planning and economic development, working under Valerie Jarrett.

- In the presidential elections on November 3, 1992, Bill Clinton defeated incumbent George H. W. Bush. Carol Moseley Braun became the first African-American woman to be elected to the US Senate, representing Illinois. Barack's Project VOTE! efforts had directly registered over 110,000 voters.

- Barack failed to meet his publishing deadline and the publisher canceled the deal, requesting he pay back his advance. Barack came up with a solution. He would spend two months finishing the book in a little cabin that his mom had rented. The only trouble was, it was 9,000 miles away in Bali. After a few months, his agent had resold the book to another publisher.

- Michelle left her job at City Hall and took a role as the executive director of the nonprofit organization Public Allies, which recruited skilled young people, trained them, and placed them in apprentice positions with community organizations and public agencies. The aim was to create the next generation of community leaders.

- Barack lost his mother, Ann Dunham, on November 7, 1995. She had been diagnosed with ovarian cancer earlier in the year and had moved from Jakarta to Honolulu for chemotherapy treatment.

- Barack was elected to the Illinois Senate in November 1996 and began commuting to the Illinois state capital, Springfield, on Mondays and returning Thursdays.

- With Public Allies thriving, Michelle took a job as associate dean focusing on community relations at the University of Chicago. She saw this as a chance to integrate the university with the city and vice versa, especially with the South Side.

JANUARY 17 BIRTHDAY QUIZ

Born on January 17, 1964 (which makes her a Capricorn in case you're interested), Michelle shares her birthday with the following ten famous figures. Can you guess them from the clues below?

1 Born in 1706, this American polymath was the inventor of the lightning rod and bifocals and one of the seven Founding Fathers.

2 This writer, born in 1820 in Yorkshire, UK, was the youngest of three sisters and penned the feminist novel *The Tenant of Wildfell Hall*.

3 Born in 1863, this politician was the first Welsh Prime Minister of the United Kingdom, occupying the position from 1916 to 1922.

4 This New York–born mobster was prosecuted in 1931 for tax evasion, for which he was sentenced to eleven years in Alcatraz.

5 This American singer was born in 1927 and famously performed the Christmas smash hit "Santa Baby" in 1953.

6 Born in 1928, this world-famous British–American hair stylist was renowned for repopularizing the "bob."

7 Born in 1931, this distinguished actor provided the voice of iconic characters Darth Vader in *Star Wars* and Mufasa in *The Lion King*.

8 Born in 1942, this legendary boxer became Heavyweight Champion of the World in 1964, at age 22, after defeating Sonny Liston.

9 Canadian–American actor born in 1962 who won a Golden Globe for his portrayal of Andy Kaufman in the film *Man on the Moon*.

10 Scottish musician born in 1984, who topped Forbes's list of the world's highest-paid DJs from 2013 to 2017.

Breadwinner See-saw

In the few years before Michelle began to work part-time in 2007 to support Barack's ambition to win the Democratic Party's nomination for president, the Obamas took turns being the primary breadwinner. Barack's advance for writing *The Audacity of Hope* and royalties for *Dreams from My Father* (1995) sneakily boosted his income in 2005 and 2006, so I'm not counting them. Judge rules Michelle wins those two years.

MICHELLE'S SALARY

2002
$98,826
(Executive director for Community Affairs at University of Chicago Hospitals)

2003
$115,889
(Executive director for Community Affairs at University of Chicago Hospitals)

2004
$121,910
(Executive director for Community Affairs at University of Chicago Hospitals)

2005
$361,962
$316,962 (Vice president for Community Affairs at University of Chicago Hospitals, where Michelle sat on the corporate board) + $45,000 (from Treehouse Foods)

2006
$324,818
$273,618 (Vice president for Community Affairs at University of Chicago Hospitals) + $51,200 (from Treehouse Foods)

BARACK'S SALARY

2002
$127,474
$69,287 (Law professor at University of Chicago) + $58,187 (Illinois state senator)

2003
$122,438
$64,287 (Law professor at University of Chicago) + $58,151 (Illinois state senator)

2004
$85,432
$32,144 (Law professor at University of Chicago) + $53,288 (Illinois state senator)

2005
$1,363,420
$154,047 (US Senator for Illinois salary) + $874,167 (as part of an advance from Random House) + $335,206 (royalties from literary agency Dystel, Goderich & Bourret)

2006
$740,200
$165,200 (US Senator for Illinois salary) + $425,000 (as part of an advance from Random House) + $150,000 (royalties from literary agency Dystel, Goderich & Bourret)

WHERE'S MICHELLE?

Can you spot our heroine (in miniature) among the vegetables?

FIRST LADY WORD SEARCH

See if you can find the first names of the past ten first ladies hidden in this word search.

BARBARA   JACKIE

HILLARY   MICHELLE

LAURA   ELEANOR

PATRICIA   LADY BIRD

BETTY   NANCY

```
Z  Z  F  J  M  N  M  B  A  G  N  Q  Y  L  N
A  I  C  I  R  T  A  P  J  N  L  F  R  A  X
S  W  D  W  D  C  L  L  A  A  D  Y  A  U  G
X  L  D  E  L  E  A  N  O  R  C  P  L  R  D
C  O  J  R  V  J  C  W  E  H  K  K  L  A  R
F  Z  K  R  I  Y  N  J  P  M  I  P  I  X  N
H  S  Z  I  Y  B  S  H  U  S  E  Q  H  E  U
Y  B  U  F  C  O  Y  M  Q  Z  M  P  B  L  C
C  S  B  O  Y  P  I  D  H  O  Z  W  A  U  J
B  I  P  T  V  C  P  A  A  X  K  R  B  J  X
I  Q  E  I  H  V  A  N  Y  L  A  L  G  S  T
S  H  G  E  P  F  Z  U  L  B  V  I  Q  H  D
X  M  L  Y  T  T  E  B  R  J  L  O  B  I  P
I  L  N  W  G  R  S  A  P  L  B  U  B  L  K
E  D  B  N  F  P  B  G  N  T  S  A  C  M  L
```

DESIGN YOUR OWN TATTOO

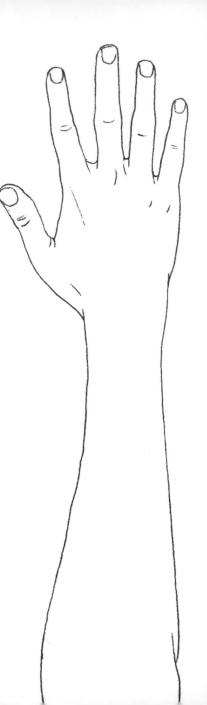

In April 2013, Barack and Michelle came up with an ingenious plan to stop Malia and Sasha from getting tattoos:

"What we've said to the girls is, 'If you guys ever decided you're going to get a tattoo, then Mommy and me will get the exact same tattoo in the same place. And we'll go on YouTube and show it off as a family tattoo."

Well, I think the Obamas can be convinced. So here's your chance to design a tattoo that they'd be impressed with.

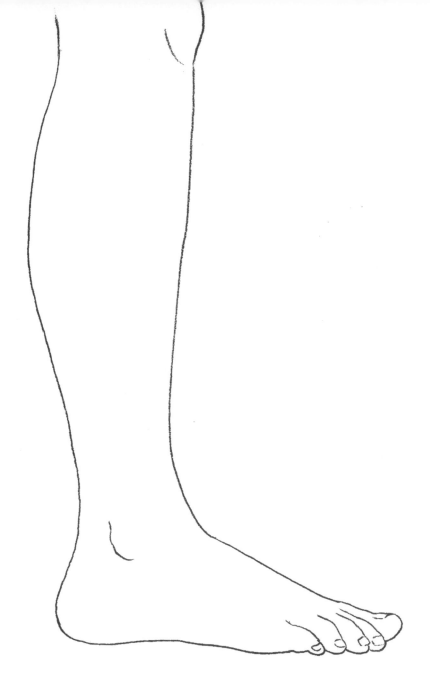

Marriage

"In our house we don't take ourselves too seriously, and laughter is the best form of unity, I think, in a marriage."

AT A WHITE HOUSE LUNCH, 2011

"When the kids go to bed and after he's done a little reading, we're usually curled up in our den, and we'll watch a show together. Or we'll talk and catch up. It's nothing major, but that's what marriage is about. Not the big, splashy stuff. It's just the little day-to-day sharing and routines and rituals that we still have."

INTERVIEW WITH *GOOD HOUSEKEEPING*, 2010

"There are a lot of young people who look at me and Barack ... and they think, 'Oh, I want those #relationshipgoals.' But I want young people to know that marriage is work. Even the best marriages require work."

TALKING TO JIMMY FALLON ABOUT MARRIAGE COUNSELLING, 2018

"We are finding each other again. We have dinners alone and chunks of time where it's just us—what we were when we started this thing: no kids, no publicity, no nothing. Just us and our dreams."

INTERVIEW WITH *PEOPLE*, 2018

"I was one of those wives who thought, 'I'm taking you to marriage counselling so you can be fixed, Barack Obama.' Because I was like, 'I'm perfect.' I was like, 'Dr X, please fix him.' And then, our counselor looked over at me. I was like, 'What are you looking at? I'm perfect!' But marriage counseling was a turning point for me, understanding that it wasn't up to my husband to make me happy, that I had to learn how to fill myself up and how to put myself higher on my priority list."

TALKING TO JIMMY FALLON ABOUT MARRIAGE COUNSELLING, 2018

On March 8, 2016, Michelle spoke to dozens of adolescent girls at Washington, DC's Union Market on behalf of the Let Girls Learn initiative to mark International Women's Day.

> "I truly see myself in these girls—in their hunger, in their burning determination to rise above their circumstances and reach for something more."

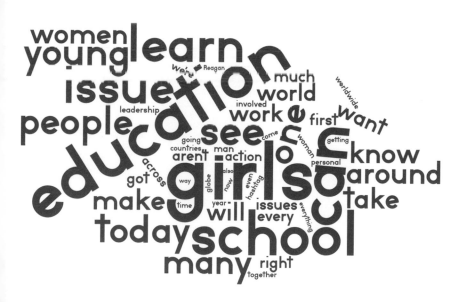

FIRST LADY OF FASHION

Here are another two of Michelle's iconic dresses, but we need you to apply the color!

She rocked this Kenzo dress in 2015 during her visit to Japan.

She wore this funky Preen by Thornton Bregazzi number in 2016 as she left Madrid.

SPOT THE DIFFERENCE

Can you spot the seven differences between this scene of the White House Vegetable Garden and the scene opposite?

Carrot "Michelle"

Carrot
"Hercules"

COLOR-IN
RELATIONSHIP GOALS

Nose Tweak

On August 4, 2016, the President and First Lady were waiting outside the White House for the arrival of the prime minister of Singapore and his wife. Michelle spotted something on Barack's nose, which she wiped off. Then, like a pair of kids in a playground, she tweaked it. Barack and Michelle: reaffirming our faith in love since 1992.

FIRST LADY
LIGHTNING
ROUND

In October 2012, Michelle appeared on morning talk show
Live with Kelly! to answer some delightfully lighthearted questions.

Dessert of choice: **"Pie."**

First job: **"Babysitting."**

Last Thing She Does before Bed:
"Pray. Kiss the girls, tuck them in."

Favorite White House Room:
"The yellow oval room."

Morning Person or Night Owl?
**"Morning person; I can't stay
awake past nine o'clock. My kids
tuck me in."**

Boxers or Briefs for the
President? **"None of the above
(she says with a smile)."**

Best Present Barack Ever Gave
Her: **"My children."**

Life of the Party or Party Pooper?
"Before nine o'clock, life of the party!"

Karaoke Song: **"Any Stevie Wonder."**

President's Karaoke Song: **"Al Green,
any Al Green, or Marvin Gaye . . . He
can sing and I can dance."**

Celebrity Crush: **"Denzel, George
Clooney, Will Smith, oh, I could
go on."**

Nickname for the President: **"Honey."**

Guilty Pleasure: **"French fries."**

Superpower: **"I would fly."**

Reality Show: **"I do love a little *Real
Housewives* every now and then."**

COPYCAT

Now I'm not sure if Michelle and Barack left all of their files and notes in First Lady Melania Trump's new office or what, but some of Melania's speeches and articles sound hauntingly familiar. I'll just leave them here and you can make your own mind up.

Below, on the left is part of Melania's *Talking with Kids About Being Online* (May 2018) booklet initially credited as "By First Lady Melania Trump and the Federal Trade Commission." The text on the left is part of the text from an Obama-era *Net Cetera: Chatting with Kids About Being Online* booklet, written in 2014.

Mobile Sharing and Networking
(2014)

Socializing and sharing on-the-go can foster creativity and fun, but could cause some problems related to personal reputation and safety.

Use care when sharing photos and videos

Most mobile phones have camera and video capability, making it easy for teens to capture and share every moment. Encourage kids to get permission from the photographer or the person in the shot before posting videos or photos. It's easier to be smart upfront about what media they share than to do damage control later.

Use good judgment with social networking from a mobile device

The filters you've installed on your home computer won't limit what kids can do on a mobile device. Talk to your teens about using good sense when they're social networking from their phones too.

Mobile Sharing and Networking
by Melania Trump (2018)

Socializing and sharing on-the-go can foster creativity and fun, but could cause some problems related to personal reputation and safety.

Use care when sharing photos and videos

Most mobile phones have camera and video capability, making it easy for teens to capture and share every moment. Encourage kids to get permission from the photographer or the person in the shot before posting videos or photos. It's easier to be smart upfront about what media they share than to do damage control later.

Use good judgment with social networking from a mobile device

The filters you've installed on your home computer won't limit what kids can do on a mobile device. Talk to your teens about using good sense when they're social networking from their phones too.

And then of course there's Melania's speech to the Republican National Convention in July 2016. Grade-A truth-teller Paul Manafort (now incidentally serving a 7½-year sentence for conspiracy to defraud the United States, witness tampering, filing false tax returns, bank fraud, and failing to disclose a foreign bank account) insisted it was "just absurd" to claim Melania had plagiarized the former First Lady, suggesting that Melania was simply "using common words".

The following day, speechwriter and Trump Organization employee Meredith McIver explained that Melania read some of the passages from Michelle's 2008 speech as examples over the phone to her. McIver wrote them down, put together a draft speech, and then forgot to alter it.

Michelle's speech to the Democratic National Convention, 2008

"…Barack and I were raised with so many of the same values: that you work hard for what you want in life; that your word is your bond and you do what you say you're going to do; that you treat people with dignity and respect …"

"… we want our children, and all children in this nation, to know that the only limit to the height of your achievement is the reach of your dreams and your willingness to work for them."

Melania Trump's speech to the Republican National Convention, 2016

"My parents impressed on me the values that you work hard for what you want in life; that your word is your bond and you do what you say and keep your promise; that you treat people with respect."

"… we want our children in this nation to know that the only limit to your achievements is the strength of your dreams and your willingness to work for them."

PRESIDENT AND FIRST LADY SHOUT-OUTS

Quite a few hip-hop and pop songs mention the great lady herself directly, or that chap she's married to.

"BO$$" by Fifth Harmony (2015)

This song mentions "Boss" Michelle in the chorus. A lot. One at-first-glance cryptic line, which I can tell you, after looking it up on Urban Dictionary, seems to refer to being on a mission to achieve a healthy body and mind (i.e. "Can't join you tonight, I'm heading to a spin class. I'm on my Michelle Obama").

"Mind On My Money" by Nicki Minaj (2009)

Nicki warns Michelle that she's got her eye on Barack. Which I suppose can either be interpreted as she's watching out for Michelle, sister-style, or exactly the opposite and she's planning to steal her man. To be honest, it's not my field of expertise.

"Forever" by Drake (2009)

Drake makes a reference to Barack Obama running the world, but he calls him "Michelle's husband" rather than Barack. So I'm taking that as an endorsement of both of them.

"Flight School" by GLC featuring Kanye West & T-Pain (2009)

This is a sort of hip-hop Romeo and Juliet/Jack and Diane/ Johnny and June reference to Barack and Michelle.

And on that note, it's fair to say that Barack gets a few independent mentions too.

"Changes" by Common (2008)

Barack is mentioned alongside Dr. Martin Luther King Jr., Gandhi, and (slightly incongruously) Shakespeare.

"On to the Next One" by Jay-Z (2009)

Barack and Jay-Z first met in 2008 on the campaign trail for the presidency, with Jay-Z and Beyoncé going on to headline numerous rallies for Barack in front of huge crowds. In this song, Jay-Z talks about having Obama "on the text." In fairness, at that point Barack had inherited an awful lot of problems (around a hundred, I think) from the previous administration and may have been seeking the rapper's help. Scandal struck when Barack disclosed on Jimmy Kimmel in 2015 that (a) he still owns a Blackberry and (b) it's essentially a child's phone with the text function disabled (although he can use email). So Jay-Z may be embellishing their day-to-day contact somewhat. But then again, he may have been talking about a point before Barack had to surrender his regular-person phone before being given the president's phone.

"Ain't No Sunshine" by Theophilus London (2009)

I'm going out on a limb here to claim that Theophilus London only mentions *llamas* because they rhyme with *Obama* in the next line. But I might have it all wrong. He might just really like llamas and *Obama* is just a rhyme of convenience.

"My President Is Black" by Jay-Z (2010)

This was originally recorded by Young Jeezy and Nas on the day that Barack secured the Democratic Party nomination for the presidency in 2008. Jay-Z added a verse for the remix, which was released on January 20, 2009, the date of Barack's inauguration. There are some truly fantastic lines, introducing hugely significant figures who pave the way for Obama, including Rosa Parks who "sat" so that Dr. Martin Luther King could "walk" so that Barack could "run." Genius.

The Birther Claim

During Barack Obama's campaign to run for President in 2008, a conspiracy theory emerged claiming that Obama was ineligible to run for office because he was not a "natural-born" citizen of the United States. People subscribing to this belief were referred to as "birthers."

"Why doesn't he show his birth certificate?... I wish he would because I think it's a terrible pall that's hanging over him ... there's something on that birth certificate that he doesn't like."

DONALD TRUMP ON DAYTIME TALK SHOW *THE VIEW*, MARCH 2011

"Growing up no one knew him ... the whole thing is very strange."

DONALD TRUMP ON *GOOD MORNING AMERICA*, MARCH 2011

On April 27, 2011, the White House released Barack Obama's long-form birth certificate. The same day, Trump claimed "victory" at "forcing" the President to release it.

"I am really honored and I am really proud, that I was able to do something that nobody else could do."

DONALD TRUMP, APRIL 27, 2011

Not content with the veracity of the birth certificate, the following year Trump tweeted:

AN "EXTREMELY CREDIBLE SOURCE" HAS CALLED MY OFFICE AND TOLD ME THAT @BARACKOBAMA'S BIRTH CERTIFICATE IS A FRAUD.

DONALD TRUMP, AUGUST 6, 2012

Finally, after Trump won the Republican Party nomination in 2016 and after several years of insisting that Barack Obama was born outside the USA, he declared:

"President Barack Obama was born in the United States. Period."

DONALD TRUMP, SEPTEMBER 16, 2016

Despite Trump's declaration the previous year, in 2017, the *New York Times* released a story revealing that he continued to embrace the birther theory privately. Shocker. Possibly not the first time the President has had trouble letting go (*quietly clears throat*: the wall, fake news, John McCain, "no collusion," using the word "great" in every sentence. I could go on, but let's face it, that's a whole other book...)

HOW THE US ELECTS A PRESIDENT

START

CONSTITUTIONAL REQUIREMENTS
To become a candidate for the Presidency, you must:

Be a natural-born citizen of the US

Be age 35 or above

Have been a resident of the US for 14 years

STEP 4
THE ELECTION
The public vote for their candidate and the votes are counted in each state. The date is statutorily set as "the Tuesday next after the first Monday in the month of November."

4

STEP 3 CAMPAIGNING
The successful party candidates tour the country to gain support. Although not constitutionally required, candidates engage in **live television debates**.

3

STEP 5 ELECTORAL COLLEGE
Each of the 50 states is allocated a number of "electors" based on the population of the state (for example, California—the most populous state—has 55 electors). There are **538** electors in total and a candidate needs to win **270** to become president.

5

STEP 1 NOMINATING A CANDIDATE

Candidates declare their intention to run for president and begin campaigning across the country.

Each state runs either a **primary** (39 states) or a **caucus** (11 states) for party members to elect a candidate.

A **caucus** involves discussion and debate at local meetings followed by an informal vote.

In a **primary**, registered voters vote via a ballot to elect the candidate they want to represent them.

Each candidate is competing for **delegates**—individuals who represent a state at the national convention.

Some states have a **winner-takes-all** mechanism, so if 51 percent of registered voters vote for a specific candidate, that candidate wins all the delegates representing that state.

Other states have a **proportional** approach whereby if a candidate wins 51 percent of the votes, they earn 51 percent of the delegates. To win the party's nomination, the candidate must win the majority of their party's delegates.

STEP 2 NATIONAL CONVENTION

Each party holds a national convention to formally select a candidate. Usually, by this point a candidate has won the required number of delegates to secure the nomination. In this case, the convention formally finalizes the party's choice. If not, a candidate is selected at the convention. The successful candidate selects a vice presidential candidate, called a **running mate**.

If a candidate wins the popular vote in a state, he or she gets **all those electoral college votes** (although some members of the college can refuse to vote for them, but this is rare). Two states, Nebraska and Maine, do not have a winner-takes-all-electoral-college-votes rule, though, so sometimes two candidates can both win electoral college votes.

STEP 6
INAUGURATION

The winning candidate is known as the **president-elect** until the inauguration on **January 20** (unless that date falls on a Sunday, in which case it is held the next day).

New Beginnings

- After negotiating unexplained fertility issues, Michelle and Barack attempted to conceive a child through in vitro fertilization (IVF). The first round was successful and Malia Ann Obama was born at the University of Chicago Medical Center on July 4, 1998.

- Barack was reelected to the Illinois State Senate in November 1998 with 89 percent of the vote. In November 2000, he challenged incumbent congressman Bobby Rush in Illinois's first congressional district election for a seat in the House of Representatives but lost.

- Natasha (Sasha) Marian Obama was born on June 10, 2001, also at University of Chicago Medical Center after a successful round of IVF.

- Michelle's former mentor and City Hall colleague, Susan Sher, suggested Michelle apply for the role of executive director for Community Affairs at the University of Chicago Medical Center, where Susan had been appointed vice president. Michelle took three-month-old Sasha to the interview, bouncing her on her lap while explaining why flexible hours would be useful. She got the job.

- In the middle of 2002, Michelle organized a brunch at Valerie Jarrett's apartment with a dozen of their close friends to discuss the idea of Barack running for Senate. Barack explained that he had a real opportunity against a struggling incumbent Republican in an increasingly Democratic state. Michelle agreed to it with one condition: if he lost, he would give up on politics.

- In the run-up to the elections, the Republican incumbent, Peter Fitzgerald, pulled out. The Democratic front-runner and the Republican nominees were both hit by scandals involving ex-wives. And then came John Kerry's offer for Barack to deliver the keynote speech to the Democratic National Convention on July 27, 2004. Michelle gave Barack a few words of advice before he went on stage:

"Just don't screw it up, buddy!"

- After seeing Barack's speech, one political commentator declared that "I've just seen the first black president." Barack won the senate election with over 70 percent of the vote.

- On May 9, 2005, Michelle was promoted to vice president for community and external affairs at the University of Chicago Medical Center.

- Hurricane Katrina struck in August 2005, leaving 1,800 people dead and 500,000 displaced. The government's inept handling of the crisis and Barack's visit to New Orleans lit a fire under Barack, making him believe that he wasn't doing enough.

- Around Christmas 2006, while visiting Barack's grandmother in Hawaii, Barack and Michelle agreed that Barack would run for president in 2008. He announced his candidacy in Springfield, Illinois, on February 10, 2007. In return, he promised Michelle he would give up smoking.

- Barack's second book, The Audacity of Hope, was published on October 17, 2006 and became a bestseller after Oprah Winfrey endorsed him for the 2008 presidential election.

COLOR-IN
RELATIONSHIP GOALS

Goofing around

The Easter Egg Roll is an annual event held on the South Lawn of the White House on Easter Monday for children age 13 or younger.

The celebration dates back to 1878 and the administration of Rutherford B. Hayes. The Egg Roll is actually a race, which involves pushing a colorful egg with a long wooden spoon while members of the administration wear Easter Bunny costumes.

FIRST LADY OF FASHION

Here are two more of Michelle's iconic dresses, but we need you to apply the color!

She wore this Roksanda fit-and flare dress on the final day of her tour to Asia in 2015.

Michelle donned this Tracy Reese floral-print dress at the Veterans Homelessness Summit in 2016.

TOP 250 MOST-FOLLOWED TWITTER ACCOUNTS AS OF MARCH 2019

1 katyperry
107,035,337

2 BarackObama
105,213,153

3 justinbieber
105,167,520

4 rihanna
90,122,706

5 taylorswift13
83,218,350

6 ladygaga
78,303,932

7 TheEllenShow (Ellen
DeGeneres)
77,229,310

8 Cristiano (Cristiano Ronaldo)
77,119,299

9 YouTube
71,329,472

10 jtimberlake
64,816,435

11 ArianaGrande
61,477,928

12 KimKardashian
60,095,499

13 realDonaldTrump
59,127,241

14 ddlovato (Demi Lovato)
57,439,469

15 selenagomez
57,287,220

16 britneyspears
56,489,699

17 Twitter
55,987,573

18 cnnbrk (CNN Breaking News)
54,891,994

19 shakira
51,059,666

20 jimmyfallon
50,908,758

21 BillGates
46,811,826

22 narendramodi (Indian Prime
Minister)
46,464,144

23 JLo
43,552,931

24 nytimes (The New York Times)
43,063,265

25 neymarjr (Neymar Jr)
42,717,796

26 BrunoMars
42,594,372

27 KingJames
(LeBron James)
42,325,953

28 Oprah (Oprah Winfrey)
42,022,571

29 MileyCyrus
41,745,950

30 CNN
41,545,020

31 NiallOfficial
(Niall Horan) 39,317,215

32 BBCBreaking
(BBC Breaking News)
39,258,199

33 Drake
38,015,514

34 iamsrk (Legendary Bollywood
actor Shah Rukh Khan)
37,696,749

35 instagram
36,688,934

36 SrBachchan (Legendary Indian
actor Amitabh Bachchan)
36,629,018

37 BeingSalmanKhan (Indian actor
Salman Khan) 36,354,681

38 SportsCenter (Flagship
program of ESPN channel)
35,290,459

39 KevinHart4real
35,038,791

40 LilTunechi (American rapper
Lil Wayne)
34,154,978

41 espn
33,794,726

42 wizkhalifa
33,715,566

43 Harry_Styles
33,279,227

44 Louis_Tomlinson
33,236,635

45 LiamPayne
32,536,540

46 Pink
31,980,656

47 realmadrid
31,640,578

48 onedirection
30,850,637

49 NASA
30,559,372

50 aliciakeys
30,002,217

51 akshaykumar
(Indian-Canadian Bollywood
actor) 29,994,650

52 chrisbrown
29,918,767

53 KAKA (Brazilian soccer player
Kaká)
29,626,459

54 kanyewest
29,321,073

55 FCBarcelona
29,276,412

56 EmmaWatson
29,097,387

57 imVkohli (Indian cricket
captain Virat Kohli) 28,829,469

58 sachin_rt (Legendary Indian
cricketer Sachin Tendulkar)
28,604,770

59 PMOIndia (official account of
the Prime Minister of India)
28,538,175

60 ConanOBrien
28,465,957

61 zaynmalik
28,215,180

62 Adele
27,846,151

63 NBA
27,700,178

64 KendallJenner
27,585,223

65 ActuallyNPH (actor Neil
Patrick Harris)
27,073,350

66 khloekardashian
26,837,840

67 KylieJenner
26,814,719

68 pitbull
(American rapper)
26,168,823

69 danieltosh
(American comedian)
26,066,585

70 deepikapadukone (Indian
actress)
25,942,097

71 POTUS (official account of the
President of the United States)
25,438,885

72 elonmusk
25,384,057

73 iHrithik
(Bollywood actor) 25,364,233

74 BBCWorld
24,749,959

75 aamir_khan
(Indian film actor)
24,566,056

76 priyankachopra
24,529,203

77 NFL
24,304,779

78 HillaryClinton
24,249,643

79 kourtneykardash
24,230,087

80 andresiniesta8
24,000,361

81 MesutOzil1088
23,866,736

82 coldplay
23,785,518

83 TheEconomist
23,615,246

84 ChampionsLeague
23,045,148

85 NatGeo (official account of
National Geographic magazine)
22,600,463

86 Eminem
22,524,389

87 AvrilLavigne
21,713,005

88 davidguetta
21,401,735

89 ShawnMendes
21,393,055

90 arrahman (Indian music director
and composer) 21,348,020

91 Google
20,891,477

92 MariahCarey
20,680,612

93 blakeshelton
20,623,167

94 MohamadAlarefe (Saudi
author, scholar and preacher)
20,529,174

95 NICKIMINAJ
20,486,167

96 ricky_martin
20,401,514

97 Reuters
20,303,480

98 AlejandroSanz
19,489,052

99 AnushkaSharma (Indian
actress) 9,192,869

100 edsheeran
19,182,888

101 premierleague
19,124,568

102 3gerardpique
19,117,659

103 DalaiLama
19,089,401

104 ManUtd
18,996,778

105 LeoDiCaprio
18,948,092

106 aliaa08 (Hindi film star Alia
Bhatt)
18,805,259

107 BTS_twt (South Koran boy
band)
18,787,730

108 Dr_alqarnee (Saudi scholar,
author and preacher)
18,730,608

109 virendersehwag (former Indian
cricketer) 18,726,866

110 FoxNews
18,534,928

111 I0Ronaldinho
18,496,430

112 StephenAtHome (US talk
show host Stephen Colbert)
18,394,502

113 JimCarrey
18,248,368

114 WhiteHouse (official account
of the White House) 18,196,428

115 jamesdrodriguez
18,151,260

116 aplusk (US actor Ashton
Kutcher)
18,032,811

117 shugairi (Saudi activist and
media figure)
17,930,390

118 Pontifex (official account of
the Pope) 17,929,022

119 GarethBale11
17,909,507

120 ALArabiya_Brk (Saudi TV news
channel)
17,885,406

121 SnoopDogg
17,642,018

122 agnezmo (Indonesian singer
and actress)
17,602,089

123 KDTrey5
(Basketball player Kevin
Durant)
17,461,390

124 ParisHilton
17,127,727

125 CNNEE (CNN en Español)
17,100,131

126 pewdiepie (Swedish YouTuber)
17,077,225

127 FALCAO (soccer player
Radamel Falcao) 17,047,457

128 WayneRooney
17,029,914

129 DaniloGentili (Brazilian
comedian)
17,023,246

130 xtina (Christina Aguilera)
16,991,464

131 Pontifex_es (official website of the Pope in Spanish) 16,939,507

132 ivetesangalo (Brazilian singer) 16,495,241

133 WSJ (The Wall Street Journal) 16,477,513

134 karanjohar (Indian film director) 16,276,918

135 PlayStation 16,151,754

136 camerondallas (US internet personality) 16,097,603

137 RyanSeacrest 16,006,359

138 ZacEfron 15,947,973

139 SergioRamos 15,933,530

140 TIME (TIME magazine) 15,851,683

141 ImRaina (Indian cricketer Suresh Raina) 15,802,525

142 radityadika (Indonesian writer) 15,743,505

143 tomhanks 15,685,565

144 RafaelNadal 15,559,886

145 MTV 15,510,475

146 LuisSuarez9 15,498,471

147 TwitterVideo 15,423,852

148 TwitterSports 15,328,560

149 paulocoelho (Brazilian novelist) 15,316,818

150 Diddy 15,289,165

151 Forbes 15,242,450

152 9GAG (Hong-Kong-based online platform) 14,998,499

153 detikcom (Indonesian online news website) 14,995,343

154 POTUS44 (archive of the official account of the Obama administration) 14,968,034

155 TwitterLatAm 14,967,208

156 Beyonce 14,900,393

157 Zendaya 14,757,092

158 SHAQ (basketball legend Shaquille O'Neal) 14,724,838

159 maroon5 14,710,073

160 tyrabanks 14,662,492

161 ArvindKejriwal (Indian politician) 14,652,313

162 jk_rowling 14,636,030

163 juniorbachchan (Indian actor Abhishek Bachchan) 14,538,724

164 VineCreators (no longer active) 14,532,225

165 BigSean (US rapper) 14,510,815

166 ClaudiaLeitte (Brazilian singer) 14,447,524

167 bts_bighit (South Korean band) 14,383,957

168 arunjaitley (Indian politician) 14,359,538

169 sonakshisinha (Indian film actress) 14,319,275

170 SethMacFarlane 14,303,003

171 enriqueiglesias 14,236,502

172 ABC 14,198,999

173 Arsenal 14,185,142

174 kobebryant 14,151,097

175 shahidkapoor (Indian actor) 14,055,008

176 nickjonas 14,006,709

177 UberFacts (Random facts app) 14,005,590

178 ALArabiya (Saudi news channel) 14,003,914

179 Alafasy (Kuwaiti preacher) 13,998,508

180 FCBarcelona_es 13,956,414

181 TreySongz (American singer, songwriter and rapper) 13,846,988

182 CMYLMZ (Turkish stand-up comedian) 13,831,736

183 funnyordie (Comedy video website) 13,831,691

184 Asli_Jacqueline (Bollywood actress) 13,677,479

185 voguemagazine 13,589,327

186 AJArabic (Al-Jazeera television network) 13,567,470

187 facebook 13,518,098

188 RT_Erdogan (Turkish President) 13,515,017

189 mangeshkarlata (Indian singer) 13,499,766

190 washingtonpost 13,484,439

191 salman_alodah (Saudi cleric) 13,473,047

192 ImRo45 (Indian cricketer Rohit Sharma) 13,397,437

193 RealHughJackman 13,337,920

194 elissakh (Lebanese singer Elissar Zakaria Khoury) 13,285,646

195 TheRock 13,282,445

196 ObamaWhiteHouse 13,281,020

197 marcosmion (Brazilian TV host) 13,262,362

198 AnupamPKher (Indian actor) 13,261,584

199 CHANEL 13,233,720

200 AP (The Associated Press) 13,224,450

201 aguerosergiokun 13,217,276

202 StephenCurry30 (US basketball player) 13,214,736

203 neiltyson (US astrophysicist) 13,172,419

204 rickygervais 13,165,520

205 Xbox 13,156,571

206 VancityReynolds (Ryan Reynolds) 13,130,604

207 NancyAjram (Lebanese singer) 13,124,779

208 ashleytisdale 13,099,977

209 KapilSharmaK9 (Indian comedian) 13,050,161

210 UberSoc (Customizable Twitter app) 12,967,978

211 AmitShah (Indian politician) 12,922,688

212 TweetRAMALAN (Indonesian astrology site) 12,905,051

213 ParineetiChopra (Indian actress) 12,897,125

214 iamwill (American musician will.iam) 12,891,674

215 CalvinHarris 12,792,890

216 victoriabeckham 12,778,166

217 stephenfry 12,724,650

218 LucianoHuck (Brazilian TV host) 12,718,128

219 ZoeSugg (English YouTuber) 12,715,643

220 sabqorg (Electronic Arabic newspaper) 12,618,375

221 Rubiu5 (Spanish YouTuber) 12,612,824

222 5SOS (Australian pop band) 12,590,977

223 SarahKSilverman (US comedian) 12,568,564

224 rajnathsingh (Indian politician) 12,565,038

225 richardbranson 12,535,299

226 johnlegend 12,523,191

227 ChelseaFC 12,521,260

228 RobertDowneyJr. 12,509,794

229 FIFAcom 12,508,754

230 JColeNC (American rapper) 12,466,447

231 sonamakapoor (Indian actress) 12,460,817

232 Jhetan_bhagat (Indian author) 12,435,641

233 rogerfederer 12,431,317

234 Usher 12,374,838

235 SushmaSwaraj (Indian politician) 12,332,196

236 CGTNOfficial (China Global Television Network) 12,325,421

237 MichelleObama 12,279,160

238 kelly_clarkson 12,261,701

239 D_DeGea (Spanish footballer) 12,151,840

240 SamsungMobile 12,071,274

2410 FarOutAkhtar (Indian film director Farhan Akhtar) 12,047,251

242 markiplier (US YouTuber) 12,046,297

243 XHNews (China Xinhua News network) 12,043,421

244 TwitterMusic 11,986,381

245 vicegandako (Filipino comedian Vice Ganda) 11,971,184

246 mindykaling (US actress) 11,879,361

247 thekiranbedi (Indian politician) 11,871,879

248 XabiAlonso 11,829,766

249 SimonCowell 11,769,746

250 RedeGlobo (Brazilian TV network) 11,737,723

Improve Donald Trump's Hollywood Star

In 2007, Donald Trump, host of *The Apprentice,* was awarded a star on Hollywood Boulevard. Then he ran for president.

To celebrate Donald's view on erecting walls, in July 2016, street artist Plastic Jesus constructed a miniature border wall around the star complete with tiny barbed-wire fencing.

In September 2016, his name was scrawled over with paint

Then, in October 2016, after a tape was released in which Trump boasted about groping women, someone took to the star with a sledgehammer. The star was subsequently covered in a protective wooden board...which was also graffitied with language probably not fit to mention here.

On May 6, 2017, a golden toilet appeared next to the star with the advisory, "Take a Trump."

In July 2018, the star was destroyed with a pickax. It was repaired, only for an anonymous street artist to frame the star with prison bars.

So, here's your opportunity to start from scratch and "improve" the design opposite any way you see fit. Give him fire and fury!

MICHELLE'S SPEECH TO THE DEMOCRATIC NATIONAL CONVENTION IN 2016

In a stirring speech to the Democratic National Convention in 2016, Michelle reflected on her husband's legacy and proudly encouraged voters to put their trust in Hillary Clinton. She did it without mentioning Donald Trump's name once, although there were several allusions to his impact on the political scene. It was a speech that instigated serious speculation about whether Michelle might run for president in the future. Here's hoping!

"Don't let anyone tell you that this country isn't great. This right now is the greatest country on earth."

DESIGN YOUR OWN
CAMPAIGN
POSTER

It's time to design your own campaign poster for Michelle, when she decides to run for president/UN secretary-general/queen/world leader.

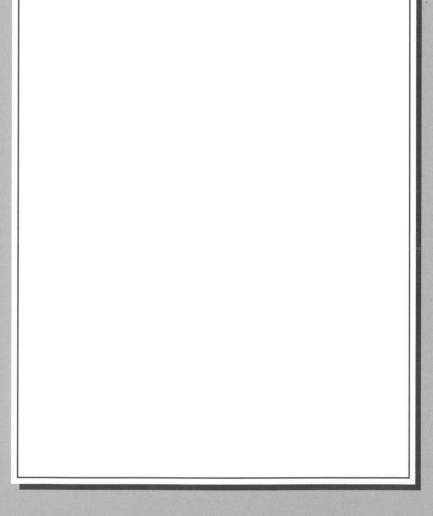

SPOT THE DIFFERENCE

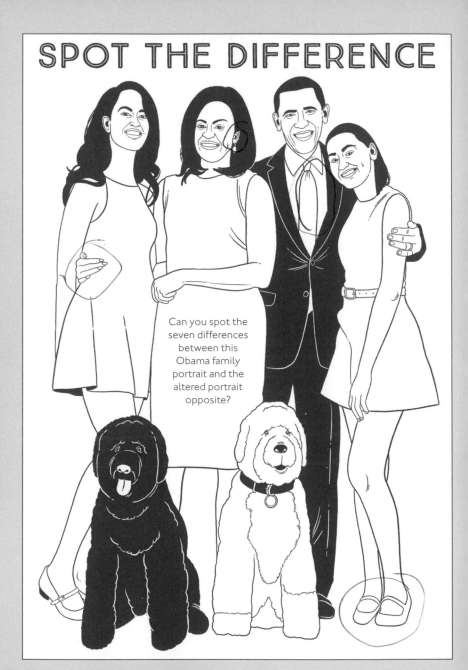

Can you spot the seven differences between this Obama family portrait and the altered portrait opposite?

Responsibility

"I've seen first hand that being president doesn't change who you are. It reveals who you are."

DEMOCRATIC NATIONAL CONVENTION, 2012

"With every word we utter, with every action we take, we know our kids are watching us. We as parents are their most important role models."

DEMOCRATIC NATIONAL CONVENTION, 2016

"Kids are watching us. I experience it every single day. They hang on my every word, what I wear, what I say."

INTERVIEW WITH *VOGUE*, 2016

"The issues that cross a president's desk are never easy. The easy questions don't even get to the president."

RALLY FOR HILLARY CLINTON AT NORTH CAROLINA STATE UNIVERSITY, 2016

"We need someone with superb judgement in their own right because, yes, a president can hire the best advisors on Earth, but I guarantee you this: Five advisors will give five different opinions. And it is the president—and the president alone—who always makes the final call."

RALLY FOR HILLARY CLINTON AT NORTH CAROLINA STATE UNIVERSITY, 2016

"If I made a commitment, I stood by that commitment—and try to make it real. Because when you become leaders, the most important thing you have is your word, your trust. That's where respect comes from."

VISIT TO R. S. CAULFIELD SCHOOL, LIBERIA, 2016

MICHELLE'S VALENTINE'S DAY PLAYLIST

For Valentine's Day 2018, Michelle put together a mixtape for Barack.
So either it's an adorable, carefully considered idea, or she forgot to get
him a present and quickly put a few songs together. Either way,
the playlist is awesome. She tweeted:

"Happy #ValentinesDay to my one and only, @BarackObama. To celebrate the occasion, I'm dedicating a little Valentine's Day playlist to you!"

To which he replied, posting a picture of the two of them on vacation:

**"Happy Valentine's Day, @MichelleObama.
You make every day and every place better."**

"Forever Mine" – Andra Day

"Stand by Me" – Ben E. King

"At Last" – Etta James

"I Found You" – Alabama Shakes

"Coming Home" – Leon Bridges

"Can't Get Enough of Your Love, Babe" – Barry White

"When Somebody Loves You Back" – Teddy Prendergrass

"The Point of It All" – Anthony Hamilton

"Endless Love" – Lionel Richie

"Keep You in Mind" – Guordan Banks

"Always and Forever" – Heatwave

"If This World Were Mine" – Luther Vandross & Cheryl Lynn

"Halo" – Beyoncé

"Fallin'" – Alicia Keys

"Lose Control" – Ledisi

"Primetime" (featuring Miguel) – Janelle Monáe

"Get You" (featuring Kali Uchis) – Daniel Caesar

"Until the End of Time" – Justin Timberlake (with Beyoncé)

"Moondance" – Van Morrison

"Maggie May" – Rod Stewart

"It's Your Love" (featuring Faith Hill) – Tim McGraw

"Every Kind of Way" – H.E.R.

"Caught Up in the Rapture" – Anita Baker

"Marry You" – Bruno Mars

"We Found Love" – Rihanna (featuring Calvin Harris)

"How Deep Is Your Love" – Calvin Harris + Disciples

"Time after Time" – Cyndi Lauper

"I Wanna Dance with Somebody (Who Loves Me)" – Whitney Houston

"Always Be My Baby" – Mariah Carey

"You and I" – Stevie Wonder

"Something in the Way She Moves" – James Taylor

"Your Song" – Elton John

"Bambi" – Jidenna

"Shape of You" – Ed Sheeran

"Just the Way You Are" – Billy Joel

"Fix You" – Coldplay

"Come Close" (featuring Mary J. Blige)– Common

"May I Have This Dance" (featuring Chance The Rapper) – Francis and the Lights

"Love" – Kendrick Lamar (featuring Zacari)

"Dog Days Are Over" – Florence and the Machine

"Bleeding Love" – Leona Lewis

"All of Me" – John Legend

Dot-to-dot Michelle

Join the dots to find Michelle with Bo, the Obamas' First Dog.

Bo was originally called New Hope by breeders Art and Martha Stern, who named him after Barack's campaign slogan in 2008. Senator Ted Kennedy gifted the dog to Sasha and Malia on April 14, 2009. The Obamas changed his name to Bo in honor of Michelle's father, who was nicknamed Diddley after legendary R&B musician Bo Diddley (1928–2008).

Parenting

"So the next time we battle with our kids over those vegetables, or they refuse to join us for a walk to the park, the next time we struggle to change our schools or communities, we need to remind ourselves that parents everywhere are going through exactly the same thing. We have to remember that we're all in this together."

LET'S MOVE! LAUNCH ANNIVERSARY, FEBRUARY 2011

"Our life before moving to Washington was filled with simple joys ... Saturdays at soccer games, Sundays at Grandma's house ... and a date night for Barack and me was either dinner or a movie, because as an exhausted mom, I couldn't stay awake for both."

DEMOCRATIC NATIONAL CONVENTION, 2012

"I love our daughters more than anything in the world, more than life itself. And while that may not be the first thing that some folks want to hear from an Ivy League–educated lawyer, it is truly who I am. So for me, being Mom-in-Chief is, and always will be, job number one."

TUSKEGEE UNIVERSITY COMMENCEMENT ADDRESS, 2015

"When a father puts in long hours at work, he's praised for being dedicated and ambitious. But when a mother stays late at the office, she's sometimes accused of being selfish, neglecting her kids."

LET GIRLS LEARN EVENT, MADRID, SPAIN, JUNE 2016

"It's about leaving something better for our kids. That's how we've always moved this country forward, by all of us coming together on behalf of our children, folks who volunteer to coach that team, to teach that Sunday school class, because they know it takes a village."

DEMOCRATIC NATIONAL CONVENTION, 2016

The famous "Hope" poster was designed by artist Shepard Fairey in 2008 with the approval of the Obama presidential campaign. I think it works just as well for Michelle.

Kiss cam

The Obamas were watching a pre-Olympics basketball match between USA and Brazil in July 2012 when they attracted the attention of the Kiss Cam on the scoreboard. Tragically, the Obamas waved to the crowd rather than smooched. Outrageous!

Undaunted, the Kiss Cam operator zoomed in on the First Couple again, and this time they gave the public what they wanted!

WHERE'S MICHELLE?

Can you spot our heroine (in miniature) among the crowd at the Democratic National Convention?

WORD CLOUD

MICHELLE'S FINAL SPEECH AS FIRST LADY

On January 6, 2017, Michelle delivered her final address as First Lady, at the 2017 School Counselor of the Year event, which she emotionally finished with:

"Being your first lady has been the greatest honor of my life, and I hope I've made you proud."

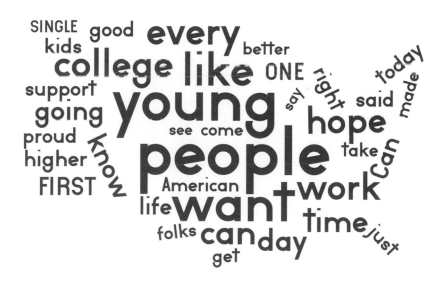

Barack on Michelle

"Anybody who knows her well knows she's got the best sense of humor of anyone you'd ever want to meet."

INTERVIEW WITH *MARIE CLAIRE*, 2008

"Obviously I couldn't have done anything that I've done without Michelle ... You were asking earlier what keeps me sane, what keeps me balanced, what allows me to deal with the pressure. It is this young lady right here ... Not only has she been a great first lady, she is just my rock. I count on her in so many ways every single day."

INTERVIEW WITH OPRAH WINFREY, 2011

"She's the most quintessentially American person I know ... She's just a wonderfully normal, level-headed person."

INTERVIEW WITH *MARIE CLAIRE*, 2008

"Well, she's very smart. She's a wonderful speaker. She's very cute. Having said all those things, the quality I love most about her is, she's honest and genuine—I think that comes across to people. They get a sense that they can trust her."

INTERVIEW WITH *LADIES HOME JOURNAL*, 2012

"If you were going to list the 100 most popular things that I have done as President, being married to Michelle Obama is number one."

AFTER HIS FIRST STATE OF THE UNION ADDRESS, 2011

"You know, the word 'authenticity' is overused these days. But I do think it captures what folks are looking for—not just in leaders, but also in friends and in coworkers—and that is, folks who are on the level. People like that tell you what they think and don't have a bunch of hidden motives. That's who Michelle is."

INTERVIEW WITH *LADIES HOME JOURNAL*, 2012

"The great thing about the girls is they've got a wonderful role model in their mom. They've seen how Michelle and I interact—not only the love but also the respect that I show to their mom. So I think they have pretty high expectations about how relationships should be, and that gives me some confidence about the future. I joke about this stuff sometimes, but the truth is they are smart, steady young women."

INTERVIEW WITH *ESSENCE* MAGAZINE, 2013

"Michelle's like Beyoncé in that song, 'Let me upgrade ya!' She upgraded me!"

INTERVIEW WITH *VOGUE*, 2013

"Incredible speech by an incredible woman. Couldn't be more proud & our country has been blessed to have her as FLOTUS. I love you, Michelle."

TWITTER, 2016

"We've been married now 20 years, and like every marriage you have your ups and you have your downs, but if you work through the tough times the respect and love that you feel deepens."

INTERVIEW WITH NEWS ANCHOR BARBARA WALTERS, 2012

"For the past 25 years, you've not only been my wife and the mother of my children, you've been my best friend. You took on a role you didn't ask for and you made it your own with grace, grit and style."

FAREWELL ADDRESS, 2017

SEAL OF THE PRESIDENT OF THE UNITED STATES

175

Michelle on Barack

"One of the things that attracted me to Barack was his emotional honesty. Right off the bat he said what he felt. There are no games with him—he is who he appears to be. I feel fortunate as a woman to have a husband who loves me and shows me [that] in every way. So yes, I do know that. And now he'll know I know."

INTERVIEW WITH *PREVENTION* MAGAZINE, 2011

"Yes, he was handsome—still is. I think so. He was charming, talented, and oh-so smart, truly. But that is not why I married him. Now, see, I want the fellas to pay attention to this. You all listening? What truly made me fall in love with Barack Obama was his character. You hear me? It was his character. It was his decency, his honesty, his compassion and conviction."

SPEECH AT MORGAN STATE UNIVERSITY, 2012

"We call it tucking. He'll come and say good night and turn the lights out and give me a kiss, and we'll talk. But I do call it—he's like, 'Ready to be tucked?' I'm like, 'Yes, I am.'"

INTERVIEW WITH *PEOPLE* MAGAZINE, 2012

"He's the same man who, when our girls were first born, would anxiously check their cribs every few minutes to ensure they were still breathing, proudly showing them off to everyone we knew. That's the man who sits down with me and our girls for dinner nearly every night, patiently answering their questions about issues in the news, and strategizing about middle-school friendships."

DEMOCRATIC NATIONAL CONVENTION, 2012

"The journey that we've taken together, the fun we've had, the challenges we've faced, the two beautiful children that we're raising—I kind of give him a pass now when he leaves his socks on the floor or tells that story for the 100th time and wants us to laugh at it as if we first heard it."

THE ELLEN DEGENERES SHOW, 2015

"It's one of many ways that Barack shows me and the girls how special we are. And that's the thing that touches me about him. I don't care what's on his plate. I don't care what he's struggling with. When he steps off that elevator into our residence he is Barack and Dad. And there's just those little things that you do that remind you, that you know, I still got ya."

THE VIEW, 2012

"Fifty-five years young and that smile still gets me every single day."

INSTAGRAM, 2016

"You can't tell it from this photo, but Barack woke up on our wedding day in October, 1992, with a nasty head cold. Somehow, by the time I met him at the altar, it had miraculously disappeared and we ended up dancing almost all night. Twenty-five years later, we're still having fun, while also doing the hard work to build our partnership and support each other as individuals. I can't imagine going on this wild ride with anybody else."

INSTAGRAM, 2018

Funny Quotes

"There's nothing more uncomfortable than asking people for stuff. I hate doing this. I love you all, but I hate asking you guys for stuff."

AT A DEMOCRATIC FUNDRAISER, NOVEMBER 2013

"What I have never been afraid of is to be a little silly, and you can engage people that way. My view is, first you get them to laugh, then you get them to listen."

INTERVIEW WITH *VARIETY*, AUGUST 2016

"Don't judge. I used to buy underwear because I didn't do my laundry."

REACH HIGHER SUMMIT, JULY 2016

"My husband will tell you one of the most frequent questions he gets from world leaders is, 'How's your wife's garden?'"

UNVEILING THE FINAL TOUCHES TO THE WHITE HOUSE VEGETABLE GARDEN, OCTOBER 2016

"I remember one parent–teacher conference at the lower school, and Barack went, and there were SWAT guys on top of the roof of the school. And Malia was like, 'Dad, really? Really? Do they really have to be up there?' And it's like, 'Yeah, honey, they do.'"

IN CONVERSATION WITH FORMER FIRST LADY LAURA BUSH AND BOB WOODRUFF, NATIONAL ARCHIVES, SEPTEMBER 2016

"Meryl Streep is exactly as awesome as you would imagine Meryl Streep to be."

SCREENING OF THE CNN DOCUMENTARY
WE WILL RISE, **OCTOBER 2016**

"Clooney is my freebie."

MICHELLE READING OUT JOKES SHE COULDN'T SAY AS FIRST LADY, *JIMMY KIMMEL LIVE*, **NOVEMBER 2018**

FINAL FAREWELL

Barack and Michelle left the White House on January 20, 2017.

On the final day of the Clinton administration, before the arrival of George W. Bush, staffers at the White House took all the "W" keys off keyboards. Now that's a good gag.

When asked by Jimmy Fallon on *The Tonight Show* what was running through her mind on the final day in the White House, Michelle quipped, **"Bye, Felisha!"** (a phrase originating in Ice Cube's 1995 film *Friday*). As Mr. Cube himself explains:

"That is the phrase to get anybody out of your face that's saying something stupid."

No prizes for guessing who she's talking about…

THE ULTIMATE
Michelle Obama Quiz

Many of the answers to the questions below appear in the book.
Now it's time to find out if you've been paying attention!

1 Which one of the following universities did Michelle NOT attend as a student?

A Harvard Law School
B Princeton
C University of Chicago

2 Michelle graduated from high school in 1981 as:

A Valedictorian (first in her class)
B Salutatorian (second in her class)
C Third in her class

3 Which grade did Michelle skip at school after her mother complained about the teacher?

A First
B Second
C Third

4 What were Michelle's words of advice for Barack before he gave the keynote speech at the Democratic National Convention?

A "Just don't screw it up, buddy!"
B "I believe in you, buddy!"
C "Go get 'em, buddy!"

5 What did Barack promise Michelle he'd give up after she supported his 2008 presidential bid?

A Alcohol
B Meat
C Smoking

6 Michelle, Hillary Clinton, and Laura Bush are the only three First Ladies to receive what?

A The Presidential Medal of Honor
B Master's degrees
C Doctorates

7 Michelle and Barack's first dance at their wedding was to which song?

A "Unforgettable" by Nat King Cole
B "You and I" by Stevie Wonder
C "White Wedding" by Billy Idol

8 The first time Michelle traveled abroad was a school trip to which country?

A Mexico
B Kenya
C France

9 Michelle became the Most Admired Woman in 2018 in Gallup's annual survey, knocking which lady off the top for the first time in seventeen years?

A Hillary Clinton
B Queen Elizabeth II
C Oprah Winfrey

10 Which American TV show host did Michelle beat in a competition to see who could do the most push-ups?

A Jimmy Kimmel
B Ellen DeGeneres
C Jimmy Fallon

11 Michelle made a surprise appearance to present an award in 2013 at which event?

A The Grammys
B The Academy Awards
C The Invictus Games

12 Michelle was joined by which singer in "Carpool Karaoke" with James Corden?

A Missy Elliott
B Beyoncé
C Jennifer Hudson

13 Michelle appears in a cameo in which popular US TV series?

A *Parks and Recreation*
B *Stranger Things*
C *The Big Bang Theory*

14 Which head of state did Michelle famously hug in 2009, which was deemed by some news outlets as a "breach of protocol"?

A The Pope
B Prince Charles
C Queen Elizabeth II

15 Which food did Michelle successfully negotiate to eat for breakfast instead of eggs?

A Peanut butter
B Porridge
C Pancakes

16 Where did Michelle and Barack go on their first official date?

A To the movies
B To a basketball match to watch the Chicago Bulls
C To a jazz club

17 Which ice cream outlet did they visit at the end of their first date?

A Ben & Jerry's
B Baskin Robbins
C Häagen-Dazs

18 What did Malia and Sasha ask for on their final night in the White House?

A Pizza and nuggets
B Burgers and fries
C Chinese food

19 What was Michelle's maternal grandfather's nickname after he moved closer to Michelle and her parents?

A Eastside
B Southside
C Northside

20 What mistake did Barack make on his first day working for Michelle's company?

A He got stuck in an elevator.
B He didn't wear a suit.
C He was late.

21 Which set of books lived on the stairwell in Michelle's apartment as a child?

A *Encyclopedia Britannica*
B *The Lord of the Rings* trilogy
C *The Chronicles of Narnia*

22 What was the make of the family car that Michelle grew up with, which her father was especially proud of?

A Chevrolet
B Buick
C Ford

23 Which fast-food outlet did Michelle and her friends hang out at in a mall in downtown Chicago on days when school got out early?

A KFC
B Burger King
C McDonald's

24 What was the name of Michelle's boyfriend, who she broke up with on the day she arrived at college?

A Ronnell
B David
C Andrew

25 Which country did Michelle make her first solo international trip to as first lady?

A Mexico
B Canada
C The United Kingdom

26 In March 2015, Michelle crossed the famous Edmund Pettus Bridge to commemorate the anniversary of the Selma–Montgomery civil rights marches. Which anniversary was it?

A 50th
B 55th
C 60th

27 How many times did it take Michelle to pass the Illinois State Bar Exam?

A One
B Two
C Three

28 Which country did Michelle and Barack travel to after they got engaged?

A Indonesia
B South Africa
C Kenya

29 Where did Barack travel to for five weeks to finish his book *Dreams from My Father*?

A Hawaii
B Nairobi
C Bali

30 Barack jokingly uttered to Michelle: "You still trying to make up your mind? Need a little more time?" before what major event?

A Agreeing to marry him
B Voting for Barack in the 2008 election
C Before placing Barack's hand on the Bible on Inauguration Day, 2009

31 What did Michelle's mother Marian famously teach Malia and Sasha how to do in the White House?

A Laundry
B Gardening
C Rewiring electric plugs

32 What alcoholic beverage was made for the first time at the White House in 2011?

A Wine
B Beer
C Gin

33 Which vegetable was omitted from Michelle's White House vegetable garden because Barack and Michelle both dislike it?

A Broccoli
B Zucchini
C Beets

34 What was famously donated to the White House vegetable garden by carpenter Charlie Brandt?

A Beehive
B Scarecrow
C Wooden sculpture of a bald eagle

35 In which city will the Barack Obama Presidential Center be housed?

A New York
B Honolulu
C Chicago

36 What was in the large blue Tiffany box that Melania Trump presented to Michelle on Inauguration Day?

A A book
B A handbag
C A picture frame

37 On March 26, 2019, Michelle's memoir *Becoming* reached a milestone, selling how many copies?

A 5 million
B 10 million
C 15 million

38 Michelle and Barack signed a joint book deal in 2017 with Penguin Random House. How much was the record advance they were paid?

A $45 million
B $55 million
C $65 million

39 Which company did the Obamas sign a deal with in May 2018, agreeing to make films and documentaries?

A Netflix
B Amazon
C Sky

40 The former "first dogs" Bo and Sunny are which breed?

A Labrador
B Poodle
C Portuguese Water Dog

41 Bo was a gift to the Obamas from which US Senator?

A Ted Kennedy
B Nancy Pelosi
C John McCain

42 In February 2017, who did Malia Obama work as an intern for?

A John Lasseter
B Brett Ratner
C Harvey Weinstein

43 Which college did Malia Obama start attending in August 2017?

A Harvard
B Yale
C Princeton

44 Sasha Obama spent her thirteenth birthday at a concert for which group?

A Maroon 5
B One Direction
C Little Mix

45 Sasha Obama was spotted doing what during Barack's 2009 inaugural address?

A Sleeping
B Yawning
C Checking her phone

46 The Obamas' dog Sunny kept getting in trouble for repeatedly doing what in the White House?

A Eating presidential papers
B Barking during meetings
C Pooing on the carpet

47 Which European country is Michelle not visiting on her Becoming book tour?

A The United Kingdom
B Germany
C France

48 Michelle's father Fraser Robinson III worked for which branch of the government for the city of Chicago?

A Water department
B Fire department
C Housing department

49 Which subject did Michelle major in at Princeton?

A International Relations
B Sociology
C African-American studies

50 What was the name of the initiative Michelle launched with Jill Biden to support military service members?

A Joining Forces
B Driving Forces
C Forces of Destiny

51 Who did Michelle meet on a trip in June 2011 that Barack admitted he was "pouty" at not being able to attend?

A Paul McCartney
B The Dalai Lama
C Nelson Mandela

52 Saudi King Abdullah presented Michelle Obama with a gift in 2009 worth $132,000. What was it?

A An antique marble clock
B An emerald tiara
C A ruby and diamond jewelry set

53 The Obamas received luxury gifts worth $41,675.71 from which European head of state in 2011?

A Nicholas Sarkozy
B Angela Merkel
C Silvio Berlusconi

54 Michelle met how many popes while she was first lady?

A One
B Two
C Three

55 Who took the most international trips as first lady?

A Hillary Clinton
B Michelle Obama
C Laura Bush

56 Michelle made an appearance on which US TV show to mark its 40th anniversary in 2009?

A *Days of Our Lives*
B *Saturday Night Live!*
C *Sesame Street*

57 The character Michelle Obama appears in an episode of *The Simpsons*, but who provided the voice?

A Oprah Winfrey
B Angela Bassett
C Beyoncé

58 Michelle turned down the chance to provide the voice for the character Michelle Obama in *The Simpsons*. What did producer James L. Brooks reveal Michelle wrote to him in a short rejection note?

A "Good try"
B "No dice"
C "No way!"

59 Which famous tourist site did Michelle, Malia, and Sasha visit in March 2014?

A Taj Mahal
B Great Wall of China
C Great Pyramid of Giza

60 Which song did not feature in Michelle's appearance on James Corden's *Carpool Karaoke*?

A "Signed, Sealed, Delivered" by Stevie Wonder
B "Single Ladies" by Beyoncé
C "Girl on Fire" by Alicia Keys

ANSWER PAGES

PAGE 15: MARK MY WORDS

The following **105** solutions exist for a total of **179** points.

agha (1 pt)	aglu (1 pt)	alae (1 pt)
alan (1 pt)	alec (1 pt)	allel (2 pts)
allice (3 pts)	alme (1 pt)	aval (1 pt)
avale (2 pts)	avel (1 pt)	cell (1 pt)
cella (2 pts)	cellae (3 pts)	celli (2 pts)
chela (2 pts)	chelae (3 pts)	cheval (3 pts)
ciel (1 pt)	cill (1 pt)	clag (1 pt)
clan (1 pt)	clave (2 pts)	clean (2 pts)
cleave (3 pts)	clem (1 pt)	clime (2 pts)
eale (1 pt)	eave (1 pt)	elan (1 pt)
eliche (3 pts)	elvan (2 pts)	emic (1 pt)
gala (1 pt)	galah (2 pts)	gale (1 pt)
galea (2 pts)	gall (1 pt)	gallic (3 pts)
gave (1 pt)	gavel (2 pts)	gleave (3 pts)
glei (1 pt)	guava (2 pts)	gula (1 pt)
gule (1 pt)	gull (1 pt)	haem (1 pt)
haemic (3 pts)	halal (2 pts)	hale (1 pt)
hall (1 pt)	hallal (3 pts)	hallan (3 pts)
hallel (3 pts)	halm (1 pt)	halva (2 pts)
halve (2 pts)	haul (1 pt)	have (1 pt)
heal (1 pt)	hell (1 pt)	ilea (1 pt)
ileal (2 pts)	lall (1 pt)	lallan (3 pts)
laugh (2 pts)	lava (1 pt)	lave (1 pt)
leal (1 pt)	lean (1 pt)	leave (2 pts)
lech (1 pt)	leva (1 pt)	lice (1 pt)
lich (1 pt)	lill (1 pt)	lime (1 pt)
meal (1 pt)	mela (1 pt)	melic (2 pts)
mell (1 pt)	mice (1 pt)	micell (3 pts)
micella (5 pts)	micellae (11 pts)	micelle (5 pts)
mich (1 pt)	miche (2 pts)	milch (2 pts)
mile (1 pt)	mill (1 pt)	mille (2 pts)
nahal (2 pts)	nala (1 pt)	nalla (2 pts)
nallah (3 pts)	naval (2 pts)	nave (1 pt)
navel (2 pts)	ugali (2 pts)	vale (1 pt)
vali (1 pt)	veal (1 pt)	vela (1 pt)

PAGES 16–17: SECRET SERVICE CODE NAME GAME

Edith Wilson	Grandma
Mamie Eisenhower	Springtime
Bess Truman	Sunnyside
Eleanor Roosevelt	Rover
Jacqueline Kennedy	Lace
Pat Nixon	Starlight
Betty Ford	Pinafore
Rosalynn Carter	Dancer
Nancy Reagan	Rainbow
Barbara Bush	Tranquility
Hillary Clinton	Evergreen
Laura Bush	Tempo
Michelle Obama	Renaissance
Melania Trump	Muse
Chelsea Clinton	Energy
Jenna Bush	Twinkle
Malia Obama	Radiance
Sasha Obama	Rosebud
Maria Shields Robinson	Raindance
Ivanka Trump	Marvel

PAGE 37: WHERE'S MICHELLE?

On the right of the picture, on the top shelf of the bookcase.

PAGE 42: WHICH FIRST LADY? QUIZ

1 C
2 A
3 D
4 C
5 A
6 D (In 1952, Nancy Davis married Ronald Reagan, who had been married to actress Jane Wyman between 1940 and 1949.)
7 C
8 A (Lady Bird Johnson owned the television station KTBC-TV/7.)
9 B
10 C

PAGES 50–51: SPOT THE DIFFERENCE

Clock on wall
Rolodex on desk
Table leg
Window
Right-hand chest of drawers
Plate on shelf
Right-hand sofa

PAGE 52: WHERE'S MICHELLE?

On the badge on Barack's jacket, hanging on the chair.

PAGE 54: WHITE HOUSE WORD SEARCH

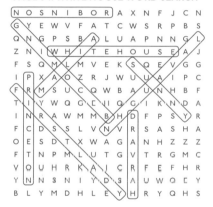

PAGES 58–59: WHITE HOUSE TRUE OR FALSE?

1. False (it was a gift from Queen Victoria)
2. True
3. True
4. True
5. False; Amy Carter, the daughter of Jimmy Carter was the only child to attend a Washington, DC public school.
6. True
7. False; she never met Lyndon B. Johnson.
8. True
9. True
10. False; it was originally called Hi-Catoctin before Franklin D. Roosevelt converted it to a presidential retreat and renamed it Shangri-La.
11. True; Air Force One is the call sign rather than the name of the Boeing VC-25 aircraft used by the president.
12. True
13. True; Frank Eugene Corder stole a Cessna 150 and crashed onto the South Lawn of the White House early on September 12, 1994, apparently trying to hit the building; he was killed in the crash.
14. True; he oversaw the building of the White House but construction was only completed in 1800 after George Washington was succeeded by the second president, John Adams.
15. False; it was added by Richard Nixon in 1969.
16. True
17. False; state dinners and official functions are paid for by the taxpayer but the president is billed at the end of every month for food, beverages, waiters, servers, and set-up and clean-up crews.
18. False; it was Winston Churchill who claimed to have seen Lincoln's ghost.
19. False; there are 132 rooms in the White House.
20. True

PAGE 60: ESCAPE THE SOCIAL EVENT MAZE

PAGE 64: NAME THAT SONG

1. "Girl on Fire"
2. "Shut up and Dance"
3. "Kiss from a Rose"
4. "Signed, Sealed, Delivered"
5. "No Diggity"

PAGE 65: SIX DEGREES OF KEVIN BACON

There are lots of ways of solving these, but the one I was thinking of was:

PERSON	FILM/TV SHOW
1. Chris Pratt	*Parks and Recreation*
2. Bradley Cooper	*Guardians of the Galaxy*
3. Christopher Walken	*Wedding Crashers*

PERSON	FILM/TV SHOW
1. Amy Poehler	*Parks and Recreation*
2. David Krumholtz	*Tenacious D in the Pick of Destiny*
3. Joseph Gordon-Levitt	*10 Things I Hate About You*

PAGE 70: MARK MY WORDS

The following **26** solutions exist for a total of **86** points.

adrift (3 pts)	drafts (3 pts)	drifty (3 pts)
eyliad (3 pts)	eyliads (5 pts)	fairly (3 pts)
filfot (3 pts)	firlot (3 pts)	flairs (3 pts)
flatus (3 pts)	floats (3 pts)	flouts (3 pts)
foliar (3 pts)	hoards (3 pts)	hoarily (5 pts)
holard (3 pts)	holards (5 pts)	lairds (3 pts)
liards (3 pts)	outfly (3 pts)	rialto (3 pts)
stairs (3 pts)	starlit (5 pts)	tailye (3 pts)
tolars (3 pts)	tufoli (3 pts)	

PAGE 76: OBAMA CROSSWORD

DOWN	ACROSS
1. Selma	3. Illinois
2. *Do the Right Thing*	5. Beyoncé
4. Fraser	6. Mexico
9. Argo	7. Prince Harry
10. Vogue	8. Basketball
12. Madrid	11. *American Grown*

PAGE 81: INAUGURATION ATTENDEE QUIZ

1. Jimmy Carter (who was born four months after George H.W. Bush)
2. Chesley Sullenberger
3. Dustin Hoffman
4. Arnold Schwarzenegger
5. Samuel L. Jackson
6. Sting
7. Miley Cyrus
8. Magic Johnson
9. Robert Zemeckis
10. John Lewis

PAGE 82: FAMOUS MICHELLES QUIZ

1. The Beatles
2. Michelle Williams
3. Michelle Pfeiffer
4. Michelle Yeoh
5. Michelle Dockery
6. Alyson Hannigan
7. Michelle Rodriguez
8. Michele Bachmann
9. Michelle Wie
10. In the asteroid belt

PAGE 90: SIX DEGREES OF KEVIN BACON

There are lots of ways of solving these, but the ones I was thinking of were:

PERSON	FILM/TV SHOW
1. Ellen DeGeneres	*The Ellen DeGeneres Show*
2. Willem Dafoe	*Finding Nemo*
3. Owen Wilson	*Fantastic Mr Fox*
4. Dick Van Dyke	*Night at the Museum*

PERSON	FILM/TV SHOW
1. Jimmy Fallon	*The Tonight Show*
2. Juliette Lewis	*Whip It*
3. George Clooney	*From Dusk Till Dawn*
4. Christopher Plummer	*Syriana*
5. Julie Andrews	*The Sound of Music*

PAGE 91: US POLITICS CROSSWORD

DOWN:	
1. Gerrymandering	9. November
2. Libertarian	ACROSS:
3. Lincoln	6. Washington
4. Camp David	8. Nine
5. White House	10. Colorado
7. Tea Party	11. Slavery
	12. Liberty

PAGES 98–99: SPOT THE DIFFERENCE

Security guard's sunglasses
Flag on car
Soldier's socks
Newspaper in car window
Badge on car

PAGE 104: FIND THE SPEECH MAZE

PAGE 105: WHERE'S MICHELLE?

On top of the chandelier.

PAGE 118: MATCH THE CHILD'S NAME TO THE FIRST FAMILY

CHILD	FIRST FAMILY
Barron	The Trumps
Chelsea	The Clintons
Jeb	The H. W. Bushes
Patti	The Reagans
Tricia	The Nixons
Caroline	The Kennedys
Jenna	The W. Bushes
Sasha	The Obamas
Lynda Bird	The Johnsons
Amy	The Carters

PAGE 119: MATCH THE FAITHFUL FRIEND TO THE FIRST FAMILY

PET	FIRST FAMILY
Sunny	The Obamas
Buddy	The Clintons
Checkers	The Nixons
Fido	The Lincolns
Faithful	The S. Grants
Fala	The D. Roosevelts
Barney	The W. Bushes
Millie	The H.W. Bushes
Liberty	The Fords
Him and Her	The B. Johnsons

PAGE 124: FIRST LADY ANAGRAMS

ARUBA LUSH = LAURA BUSH
PLATINUM MARE = MELANIA TRUMP
CHILLY TORN NAIL = HILLARY CLINTON
HOOVERED TILES = EDITH ROOSEVELT
PAN TOXIN = PAT NIXON
ABLE CHAMOMILE = MICHELLE OBAMA
BAA RHUBARBS = BARBARA BUSH
ANNY CARNAGE = NANCY REAGAN
CINDY JAKE KEEN = JACKIE KENNEDY
DERBY TOFT = BETTY FORD
ELEVATOR LOOSENER = ELEANOR ROOSEVELT
MARATHONS THAWING = MARTHA WASHINGTON

PAGE 128: JANUARY 17 BIRTHDAY QUIZ

1. Benjamin Franklin
2. Anne Brontë
3. David Lloyd George
4. Al Capone
5. Eartha Kitt
6. Vidal Sassoon
7. James Earl Jones
8. Muhammad Ali
9. Jim Carrey
10. Calvin Harris

PAGE 130: WHERE'S MICHELLE?

In the left-hand basket of vegetables.

PAGE 131: FIRST LADY WORD SEARCH

```
Z Z F J M N M B A G N Q Y L N
A I C I R T A P J N L F R A X
S W D W D C L L A A D Y A U G
X L D E L E A N O R C P L R D
C O J R V J C W E H K K L A R
E Z K R Y N J P M I P I X N
H S Z I Y B S H U S E Q H E U
Y B U F C O Y M Q Z M P B L C
C S B O Y P D H O Z W A U J
B I P T V C P A A X K R B J X
I Q E I H V A N Y L A L G S T
S H G E P F Z U L B V I Q H D
X M L Y T T E B R J L O B I P
I L N W G R S A P L B U B L K
E D B N F P B G N T S A C M L
```

PAGE 138–139: SPOT THE DIFFERENCE

Flag
Lettuce
Michelle's belt
Trowel
Plant label

PAGE 153: WHERE'S MICHELLE?

Next to the 'Outraged' banner, center bottom of picture.

PAGES 164–165: SPOT THE DIFFERENCE

Malia's earring
Michelle's hand
Michelle's earring
Barack's tie
Barack's pocket
Sasha's shoes
Dog's collar

PAGE 172: WHERE'S MICHELLE?

Center right, above banner

PAGES 181–185: THE ULTIMATE MICHELLE OBAMA QUIZ

1 C	25 A	49 B
2 B	26 A	50 A
3 B	27 B	51 C
4 A	28 C	52 C
5 C	29 C	53 A
6 B	30 B	54 B
7 A	31 A	55 A
8 C	32 B	56 C
9 A	33 C	57 B
10 B	34 A	58 A
11 B	35 C	59 B
12 A	36 C	60 C
13 A	37 A	
14 C	38 C	
15 A	39 A	
16 A	40 C	
17 B	41 A	
18 A	42 C	
19 B	43 A	
20 C	44 B	
21 A	45 B	
22 B	46 C	
23 C	47 B	
24 B	48 A	

ACKNOWLEDGMENTS

First and foremost to the great lady herself.
A true inspiration to so many.

Tarah, another great lady, sounding board, selfless mood-improver, and for always telling me to look upwards.

Thanks to **Nicola** for your support and faith, **Michelle**, **Sally** and **Manjit** for all your hard work, and **Milner** for your reassurance and encouragement. A big thank you to **Tina** and **David** for your continued belief.

Thank you, **Toby Triumph**, whose designs live up to his name and for putting up with that gag, which he definitely hasn't heard before.

To my wonderful niece **Zsófia Joyce** for beginning to write her own versions of my books. I don't think anyone's ever written an unofficial version of an unofficial book before. My lawyer will be in touch shortly.

Lastly to my **mum** (thanks, mum!) for buying at least several hundred copies of each book I write.